Birth Control

A Statement of Christian Doctrine against the Neo-Malthusians

by

Halliday G. Sutherland

Arcadia
MMXVIII

Printed in the United States of America

ISBN 978-1-944339-11-1

Birth Control

Published by Tumblar House
Visit our website at www.tumblarhouse.com

TABLE OF CONTENTS

FOREWORD 1
CHAPTER 1 5
THE ESSENTIAL FALLACIES OF MALTHUSIAN TEACHING 5
  §1. MALTHUS AND THE NEO-MALTHUSIANS 5
  §2. TEACHING BASED ON FALSE PREMISES 7
  §3. THE ROOT FALLACY 9
  §4. WHAT OVERPOPULATION MEANS 10
  §5. NO EVIDENCE OF OVERPOPULATION 11
  §6. A NATURAL LAW CHECKING FERTILITY 13
  §7. OVERPOPULATION IN THE FUTURE 14
  §8. HOW NATIONS HAVE PERISHED 15
  §9. PHYSICAL CATASTROPHES 15
  §10. MORAL CATASTROPHES 19
CHAPTER 2 21
THE FALSE DEDUCTIONS CONCERNING POVERTY 21
  §1. BIRTH-RATE AND POVERTY 21
  §2. POVERTY IN GREAT BRITAIN DUE TO OTHER CAUSES 24
  §3. CAUSES OF POVERTY IN INDIA 26
  §4. POVERTY IN FACT CAUSES A HIGH BIRTH-RATE 27
  §5. POVERTY AND CIVILISATION 30

CHAPTER 3 32
HIGH BIRTH-RATES NOT THE CAUSE OF HIGH
  DEATH-RATES 32
  §1. POVERTY AS NOW EXISTING 32
  §2. HIGH BIRTH-RATE NOT THE CAUSE OF HIGH
  DEATH-RATE: PROVED FROM STATISTICS 33
  §3. A LOW BIRTH-RATE NO GUARANTEE OF A
  LOW DEATH-RATE 34
  §4. VITAL STATISTICS OF FRANCE 35
  §5. COEFFICIENTS OF CORRELATION 37
CHAPTER 4 40
HOW RELIGION AFFECTS THE BIRTH-RATE 40
  §1. FRENCH STATISTICS MISINTERPRETED BY
  MALTHUSIANS 40
  §2. EVIDENCE FROM HOLLAND 44
  §3. THE UNITED STATES OF AMERICA 45
  §4. THE SAME RESULTS IN ENGLAND 48
CHAPTER 5 54
IS THERE A NATURAL LAW REGULATING THE
  PROPORTION OF BIRTHS AND DEATHS? 54
  §1. THE THEORY OF THOMAS DOUBLEDAY
  REVIVED 54
  §2. MR. PELL'S GENERALISATIONS CRITICISED
  55
  §3. THE LAW OF DECLINE 57
  §4. ILLUSTRATED FROM GREEK HISTORY 58
CHAPTER 6 62
THE FALLING BIRTH-RATE IN ENGLAND: ITS
  CAUSES 62

§1. NOT, AS MALTHUSIANS ASSERT, DUE MAINLY TO CONTRACEPTIVES 62
§2. DECLINE IN FERTILITY DUE TO SOME NATURAL LAW 64
§3. AND TO CHARACTER OF OCCUPATION 66
§4. AGGRAVATED DOUBTLESS BY MALTHUSIANISM 67
CHAPTER 7 68
THE EVILS OF ARTIFICIAL BIRTH CONTROL 68
§1. NOT A PHYSICAL BENEFIT 68
§2. A SCANDALOUS SUGGESTION 72
§3. A CAUSE OF UNHAPPINESS IN MARRIAGE . 76
§4. AN INSULT TO TRUE WOMANHOOD 77
§5. A DEGRADATION OF THE FEMALE SEX 79
§6. SPECIALLY HURTFUL TO THE POOR 81
§7. A MENACE TO THE NATION 83
§8. THE PLOT AGAINST CHRISTENDOM 94
CHAPTER 8 99
THE RELIGIOUS ARGUMENT AGAINST BIRTH CONTROL 99
§1. AN OFFENCE AGAINST THE LAW OF NATURE 99
§2. REFLECTED IN THE NORMAL CONSCIENCE 100
§3. EXPRESSED IN THE SCIENCE OF ETHICS ... 101
§4. BIRTH CONTROL CONDEMNED BY PROTESTANT CHURCHES 102
APPENDIX TO CHAPTER 8 105
A NEO-MALTHUSIAN ATTACK ON THE CHURCH OF ENGLAND 105

CHAPTER 9 117
THE TEACHING OF THE CATHOLIC CHURCH ON
    BIRTH CONTROL 117
  §1. A FALSE VIEW OF HER DOCTRINE 117
  §2. THE ESSENCE AND PURPOSE OF MARRIAGE
    118
  §3. ARTIFICIAL STERILITY WHOLLY
CONDEMNED 119
  §4. THE ONLY LAWFUL METHOD OF BIRTH
CONTROL 120
  §5. CONCLUSION 122
BIBLIOGRAPHY 124
APPENDIX: *HUMANAE VITAE* 128

FOREWORD

By Charles A. Coulombe

IN A SOCIETY BASED ON LIES, tellers of truth must pay the price for their veracity. Sometimes this price is paid with suffering whilst they live; at other, the penalty is obscurity after death, no matter how accomplished they may have been, howsoever heroic or helpful to their fellow man they may have been. The latter punishment was meted out to Halliday Sutherland (1882-1960), the author of this book.

His travel books first came to my attention when I was in High School—there were copies of his *Lapland Adventure* and *Hebridean Adventure* in my school library. His skillful and vivid writing brought those remote places alive to the reader—as did his appreciation for the local folklore. Later, I discovered that he was a Catholic convert, and that Chesterton himself had lauded his work, saying "Dr. Halliday Sutherland is a born writer, especially a born story-teller. Dr. Sutherland, who is distinguished in medicine, is an amateur in the sense that he only writes when he has nothing better to do. But when he does, it could hardly be done better." Indeed.

It turned out that his medical career was indeed distinguished. Becoming a doctor in 1908, the newly minted Dr. Sutherland would go to hold a number of distinguished positions in his chosen profession. But he chose in particular what was then a devastating medical enemy: tuberculosis. At the time, the disease was rife among Britain's poor. Partly it was because of the appalling conditions under which so many of them lived, and partly because the then common treatment—sending the sufferer off to recover, if possible, at a resort-like sanatorium in a healthier climate—was quite simply beyond the means of the disease's poorer victims. But there were other factors, such as the sale of cheap tuberculous milk to the poverty stricken, and its consumption by their children. In combating this plague, he came up against resistance from the then popular eugenics lobby.

Although few people would openly admit to espousing eugenics today, thanks to Nazi support for it rendering it less than respectable (although one still hears private complaints about various groups "breeding like rabbits"), it was quite popular among what passed for the educated circles in North America and Europe before and after World War I. Thus, in his article on "Civilization" in the 1911 *Encyclopaedia Britannica*, American physician Dr. Henry Smith Williams could blithely write:

> Equally obvious must it appear to the cosmopolite of some generation of the future that quality rather than mere numbers must determine the efficiency of any given community. Race suicide will then cease to be a bugbear; and it will no longer be considered rational to keep up the census at the cost of propagating low orders of intelligence, to feed the ranks of paupers, defectives and criminals. On the contrary it will be thought fitting that man should become the conscious arbiter of his own racial destiny to the extent of applying whatever laws of heredity he knows or may acquire in the interests of his own species, as he has long applied them in the case of domesticated animals.

Dr. Sutherland soon realized that the eugenists opposed any efforts to reduce tuberculosis among the poor. By the time he began to speak out publicly against the Eugenics lobby in 1917, 10,000 British children were dying of the disease a year—due in no small part to the tainted milk mentioned earlier. At that time one of Britain's leading eugenists declared that the disease was "a rough, but on the whole very serviceable check, on the survival and propagation of the unfit."

Early on, Dr. Sutherland discovered that foremost among the holders of this position were the advocates of artificial contraception. Of the most notable of these were the American Margaret Sanger and the British Marie Stopes. Both saw their work as a way of eliminating the unfit—a position that led Mrs. Sanger to be endorsed by both the Nazis and the Ku-Klux-Klan. As a result, Dr. Sutherland opposed the practice on both ethical and moral grounds.

In 1922, Dr. Sutherland wrote *Birth Control: A Statement of Christian Doctrine against the Neo-Malthusians*—the book you are about to read. He had just converted to Catholicism, a move which strengthened his pre-existing views. Amongst other things, he exposed the eugenics interests of Mrs. Stopes, to which she did not react well. She sued Dr. Sutherland for libel, was defeated in the first court, upheld on appeal, and at last was defeated in the House of Lords. There was no libel, only a blunt description of the issues involved and the motivations of the birth control adherents. But he ended the book with a statement that—seen from 2018—was chillingly prophetic:

> Our declining birth-rate is a fact of the utmost gravity, and a more serious position has never confronted the British people. Here in the midst of a great nation, at the end of a victorious war, the law of decline is working, and by that law the greatest empires in the world have perished. In comparison with that single fact all other dangers, be they of war, of politics, or of disease, are of little moment. Attempts have already been made to avert the consequences by the partial endowment of motherhood and by a saving of infant life. Physiologists are now seeking among the endocrinous glands and the vitamins for a substance to assist procreation. 'Where are my children?' was the question shouted yesterday from the cinemas. 'Let us have children, children at any price,' will be the cry of tomorrow.

Foreign labour and women in the military are the means our masters have employed to attempt to make up for the population implosion in Europe and North America.

This edition is part of the commemoration of the 50th anniversary of Bl. Pope Paul's encyclical, *Humanae Vitae*. As with Dr. Sutherland, Paul VI was aware of the danger to humanity artificial contraception posed; similarly, in its pages he prophesied exactly how the relationship between the sexes would disintegrate. Here again, from our perspective he seems like a wildly successful fortune teller—just like Dr. Sutherland.

Mention must be made here of the Halliday Sutherland website (https://hallidaysutherland.com) maintained by his Australian grandson, Mark Sutherland. The younger Mr. Sutherland must congratulated on his yeoman efforts in reviving his illustrious forebear's name and work. Far better able to introduce the reader to Dr. Sutherland's life and work than a short foreword could ever be, it is heartily recommended to the reader. As with *Humanae Vitae*, may the good doctor's work find a hoe in the hearts of the rising generation. Dr. Sutherland's views—on this and a great many other things—have never been more needed than to-day.

    Charles A. Coulombe
    Monrovia, California
    July 25, 2018
    Feast of St. James the Great

CHAPTER 1
THE ESSENTIAL FALLACIES OF MALTHUSIAN TEACHING

§1. MALTHUS AND THE NEO-MALTHUSIANS

BIRTH CONTROL, in the sense of the prevention of pregnancy by chemical, mechanical, or other artificial means, is being widely advocated as a sure method of lessening poverty and of increasing the physical and mental health of the nation. It is, therefore, advisable to examine these claims and the grounds on which they are based. The following investigation will prove that the propaganda throughout Western Europe and America in favour of artificial birth control is based on a mere assumption, bolstered up by economic and statistical fallacies; that Malthusian teaching is contrary to reason and to fact; that Neo-Malthusian practices are disastrous alike to nations and to individuals; and that those practices are in themselves an offence against the Law of Nature, whereby the Divine Will is expressed in creation.

(a) Malthus

The Rev. Thomas Malthus, M.A.., in 1798 published his Essay on the Principle of Population. His pamphlet was an answer to Condorcet and Godwin, who held that vice and poverty were the result of human institutions and could be remedied by an even distribution of property. Malthus, on the other hand, believed that population increased more rapidly than the means of subsistence, and consequently that vice and poverty were always due to overpopulation and not to any particular form of society or of government. He stated that owing to the relatively slow rate at which the food supply of countries was increased, a high birth-rate[1] inevitably led to all the evils of poverty, war, and high death-rates. In an infamous passage he wrote that there was no vacant place for the superfluous child at Nature's mighty feast; that Nature told the child to be gone; and that she quickly executed her own order. This passage was modified in the second, and deleted from the third edition of the Essay. In later editions he maintained that vice and misery had checked population, that the progress of society might have diminished rather than increased the "evils resulting from the principle of population," and that by "moral restraint" overpopulation could be prevented. As Cannan has pointed out,[2] this last suggestion destroyed the force of the argument against Godwin, who could have replied that in order to make "moral restraint" universal a socialist State was necessary. In order to avoid the evils of overpopulation, Malthus advised people not to marry, or, if they did, to marry late in life and to limit the number of their children by the exercise of self-restraint. He reprobated all artificial and unnatural methods of birth control as immoral, and as removing the necessary stimulus to industry; but he failed to grasp the whole truth that an increase of population is necessary as a stimulus not only to industry, but also as essential to man's moral and intellectual progress.

(b) The Neo-Malthusians

The Malthusian League accept the theory of their revered teacher, but, curiously enough, they reject his advice "as being impracticable and productive of the greatest possible evils to health and morality."[3] On the contrary, they advise universal early marriage, combined with artificial birth control. Although

---

[1] The birth-rate is the number of births per 1,000 of the whole population. In order to make a fair comparison between one community and another, the birth-rate is often calculated as the number of births per 1,000 married women between 15 and 45 years of age, as these constitute the great majority of child-bearing mothers. This is called the *corrected birth-rate*.

[2] *Economic Review*, January 1892.

[3] So says the Secretary of the Malthusian League. Vide *The Declining Birth-rate*, 1916, p. 88.

their policy is thus in flat contradiction to the policy of Malthus, there are two things common to both. Each is based on the same fallacy, and the aim of both is wide of the mark. Indeed, the Neo-Malthusian, like Malthus, has "a mist of speculation over his facts, and a vapour of fact over his ideas."[4] Moreover, as will be shown here, the path of the Malthusian League, although at first glance an easy way out of many human difficulties, is in reality the broad road along which a man or a nation travels to destruction; and as guides the Neo-Malthusians are utterly unsafe, since they argue from (*a*) false premises to (*b*) false deductions. We shall deal with the former in this chapter.

§2. TEACHING BASED ON FALSE PREMISES

The theory of Malthus is based on three errors, namely (*a*) that the population increases in geometrical progression, a progression of 1, 2, 4, 8, 16, and so on upwards; (*b*) that the food supply increases in arithmetical progression, a progression of 1, 2, 3, 4, 5, and so on upwards; and (*c*) that overpopulation is the cause of poverty and disease. If we show that *de facto* there *is* no overpopulation it obviously cannot be a cause of anything, nor be itself caused by the joint operation of the first two causes. However, each of the errors can be severally refuted.

(*a*) In the first place, it is true that a population *might* increase in geometrical progression, and that a woman *might* bear thirty children in her lifetime; but it is wrong to assume that because a thing *might* happen, it therefore does happen. The population, as a matter of fact, does not increase in geometrical progression, because Nature[5] places her own checks on the birth-rate, and no woman bears all the children she might theoretically bear, apart altogether from artificial birth control.

---

[4] Bagehot, *Economic Studies*, p. 193.
[5] To assign a personality to "Nature" is, of course, a mere *façon de parler*; the believer holds that the "course of Nature" is an expression of the Mind and Will of the Creator.

(*b*) Secondly, the food supply does not of necessity increase in arithmetical progression, because food is produced by human hands, and is therefore increased in proportion to the increase of workers, unless the food supply of a country or of the world has reached its limit. The food supply of the world *might* reach a limit beyond which it could not be increased; but as yet this event has not happened, and there is no indication whatsoever that it is likely to happen.

Human life is immediately sustained by food, clothing, shelter, and fuel. Food and clothing are principally derived from fish, fowl, sheep, cattle, and grain, all of which *tend*, more so than man, to increase in *geometrical* ratio, although actually their increase in this progression is checked by man or by Nature. As regards shelter there can be no increase at all, either arithmetical or geometrical, apart from the work of human hands. Again, the stock of fuel in or on the earth cannot increase of itself, and is gradually becoming exhausted. On the other hand, within living memory, new sources of fuel, such as petroleum, have been made available, and old varieties of fuel have been used to better advantage, as witness the internal-combustion engine driven by smoke from sawdust. Moreover, in the ocean tides is a vast energy that one day may take the place of fuel.

(*c*) Thirdly, before anyone can reasonably maintain that overpopulation is the cause of poverty and disease, it is necessary to prove that overpopulation actually exists or is likely to occur in the future. By overpopulation we mean the condition of a country in which there are so many inhabitants that the production of necessaries of livelihood is insufficient for the support of all, with the result that many people are overworked or ill-fed. Under these circumstances the population can be said to *press on the soil*: and unless their methods of production could be improved, or resources secured from outside, the only possible remedy against the principle of diminishing returns would be a reduction of population; otherwise, the death-rate from want and starvation would gradually rise until it equalled the birth-rate in order to maintain an unhappy equilibrium.

§3. THE ROOT FALLACY

According to Malthusian doctrine overpopulation is the cause of poverty, disease, and war: and consequently, unless the growth of population is artificially restrained, all attempts to remedy social evils are futile. Malthusians claim that "if only the devastating torrent of children could be arrested for a few years, it would bring untold relief." They hold that overpopulation is the root of all social evil, and the truth or falsehood of that proposition is therefore the basis of all their teaching. Now, when Malthusians are asked to prove that this their basic proposition is true, they adopt one of two methods, not of proof, but of evasion. Their first method of evading the question is by asserting that the truth of their proposition is self-evident and needs no proof. To that we reply that the falsity of the proposition can and will be proved. Their second device is to put up a barrage of facts which merely show that all countries, and indeed the earth itself, would have been overpopulated long ago if the increase of population had not been limited by certain factors, ranging from celibacy and late marriages to famines, diseases, wars, and infanticide. The truth of these facts is indisputable, but it is nevertheless a manifest breach of logic to argue from the fact of poverty, disease, and war having checked an increase of population, that therefore poverty, disease, and war are due to an increase of population. It would be as reasonable to argue that, because an unlimited increase of insects is prevented by birds and by climatic changes, therefore an increase of insects accounts for the existence of birds, and for variations of climate. Nor is it of any use for Malthusians to say that overpopulation *might* be the cause of poverty. They cannot prove that it *is* the cause of poverty, and, as will be shown in the following chapter, more obvious and probable causes are staring them in the face. For our present purpose it will suffice if we are able to prove that overpopulation has not occurred in the past and is unlikely to occur in the future.

§4. WHAT OVERPOPULATION MEANS

In the first place, the meaning of the word "overpopulation" should be clearly understood. The word does not mean a very large number of inhabitants in a country. If that were its meaning the Malthusian fallacy could be disproved by merely pointing out that poverty exists both in thinly populated and in thickly populated countries. Now, in reality, overpopulation would occur whenever the production of the necessities of life in a country was insufficient for the support of all the inhabitants. For example, a barren rock in the ocean would be overpopulated, even if it contained only one inhabitant. It follows that the term "overpopulation" should be applied only to an economic situation in which the population presses on the soil. The point may be illustrated by a simple example.

Let us assume that a fertile island of 100 acres is divided into 10 farms, each of 10 acres, and each capable of supporting a family of ten. Under these conditions the island could support a population of 1,000 people without being overpopulated. If, however, the numbers in each family increased to 20 the population would *press on the soil*, and the island, with 2,000 inhabitants, would be an example of overpopulation, and of poverty due to overpopulation.

On the other hand, let us assume that there are only 1,000 people on the island, but that one family of ten individuals has managed to gain possession of eight farms, in addition to their own, and that the other nine families are forced to live on one farm. Obviously, 900 people would be attempting to live under conditions of dire poverty, and the island, with its population of 1,000, would now offer an excellent example, not of overpopulation, but of human selfishness.

My contentions are that poverty is neither solely nor indeed generally related to economic pressure on the soil; that there are many causes of poverty apart altogether from overpopulation; and that in reality overpopulation does not exist in those countries where Malthusians claim to find proofs of social misery due to a high birth-rate.

If overpopulation in the economic sense occurred in a closed country, whose inhabitants were either unable or unwilling to send out colonies, it is obvious that general poverty and misery would result. This *might* happen in small islands, but it is of greater interest to know what does happen.

§5. NO EVIDENCE OF OVERPOPULATION

In a closed country, producing all its own necessities of life and incapable of expansion, a high birthrate would eventually increase the struggle for existence and would lead to overpopulation, always provided that, firstly, the high birth-rate is accompanied by a low death-rate, and secondly, that the high birth-rate is maintained. For example, although a birth-rate was high, a population would not increase in numbers if the death-rate was equally high. Therefore, a high birth-rate does not of necessity imply that population will be increased or that overpopulation will occur. Again, if the birth-rate fell as the population increased, the danger of overpopulation would be avoided without the aid of a high death-rate. For a moment, however, let us assume that the Malthusian premise is correct, that a high birth-rate has led to overpopulation, and that the struggle for existence has therefore increased. Then obviously the death-rate would rise; the effect of the high birth-rate would be neutralised; and beyond a certain point neither the population nor the struggle for existence could be further increased. On these grounds Neo-Malthusians argue that birth-control is necessary precisely to obviate that cruel device whereby Nature strives to restore the balance upset by a reckless increase of births; and that the only alternative to frequent and premature deaths is regulation of the source of life. As a corollary to this proposition they claim that, if the death-rate be reduced, a country is bound to become overpopulated unless the births are artificially controlled. Fortunately it is possible to test the truth of this corollary, because certain definite observations on this very point have been recorded. These observations do not support the argument of birth controllers.

(a) In the Suez Canal Zone

In the Suez Canal Zone there was a high death-rate chiefly owing to fever. According to Malthus it would have been a great mistake to lower this death-rate, because, if social conditions were improved, the population would rapidly increase and exceed the resources of the country. Now, in fact, the social conditions were improved, the death-rate was lowered, and the subsequent events, utterly refuting the above contention, are thus noted by Dr. Halford Ross, who was medical officer in that region:

> During the years 1901 to 1910, health measures in this zone produced a very considerable fall in the death-rate, from 30.2 per thousand to 19.6 per thousand; the infant mortality was also reduced very greatly, and it was expected that, after a lapse of time, the reduction of the death-rate would result in a rise of the birth-rate, and a corresponding increase of the population. *But such was not the case.* When the death-rate fell, the birth-rate fell too, and the number of the population remained the same as before, even after nearly a decade had passed, and notwithstanding the fact that the whole district had become much healthier, and one town, Port Said, was converted from an unhealthy, fever-stricken place into a seaside health resort.[6]

Moreover, Dr. Halford Ross has told me that artificial birth control was not practised in this region and played no part in maintaining a stationary population. The majority of the people were strict Mohammedans, amongst whom the practice of birth control is forbidden by the Koran.

(b) In "Closed Countries" like Japan

But a much more striking example of the population in a closed country remaining stationary without the practice of birth control, thus refuting the contention of our birth controllers, is to be found in their own periodical, *The Malthusian*.[7] It would

---

[6] *Problems of Population*, p. 382.
[7] *The Malthusian*, July 15, 1921.

appear that in Japan from 1723 to 1846 the population remained almost stationary, only increasing from 26,065,422 to 26,907,625. In 1867 the Shogunate was abolished, the Emperor was restored, and Japan began to be a civilised power. Now from 1872 the population increased by 10,649,990 in twenty-seven years, and "during the period between 1897 and 1907 the population received an increment of 11.6 percent, whereas the food-producing area increased by only 4.4 percent. ... According to Professor Morimoro, the cost of living is now so high in Japan that 98 percent of the people do not get enough to eat." From these facts certain obvious deductions may be made. So long as Japan was a closed country her population remained stationary. When she became a civilised industrial power the mass of her people became poorer, the birth-rate rose, and the population increased, this last result being the real problem today in the Far East. In face of these facts it is sheer comedy to learn that our Malthusians are sending a woman to preach birth control amongst the Japanese! Do they really believe that for over a hundred years Japan, unlike most semi-barbaric countries, practised birth control, and that when she became civilised she refused, unlike most civilised countries, to continue this practice? There is surely a limit to human credulity.

The truth appears to be that in closed countries the population remains more or less stationary, that Nature herself checks the birth-rate without the aid of artificial birth control, and that birth-rates and death-rates are independently related to the means of subsistence.

§6. A NATURAL LAW CHECKING FERTILITY

During the past century the population of Europe increased by about 160,000,000, but it is utterly unreasonable to assume that this rate of increase will be maintained during the present century. It would be as sensible to argue that because a child is four feet high at the age of ten he will be eight feet high at the age of twenty. Moreover, there is evidence that, apart altogether from vice, the fertility of a nation is reduced at every step in civilisation. The cause of this reduction in fertility is unknown. It is probably a reaction to many complex influences, and possibly associated with the vast growth of great cities. This decline in the fertility of a community is a natural protection against the possibility of overpopulation; but, on the other hand, there is a point beyond which any further decline in fertility will bring a community within sight of depopulation and of extinction.

§7. OVERPOPULATION IN THE FUTURE

It is a fallacy to say that overpopulation is the cause of poverty and disease, and that for the simple reason that overpopulation has not yet occurred. For the growth of a nation we assume that the birth-rate should exceed the death-rate by from 10 to 20 per thousand, and it is obvious that in a *closed* country the evil of overpopulation might appear in a comparatively short time. The natural remedies in the past have been emigration and colonisation. According to the birth controllers these remedies are only temporary, because sooner or later all colonies and eventually the earth itself will be overpopulated. At the British Association Meeting in 1890 the population of the earth was said to be 1,500 millions, and it was calculated that only 6,000 millions could live on the earth. This means that if the birth-rate throughout the world exceeded the death-rate by only 8 per thousand, the earth would be overpopulated within 200 years. It is probable that in these calculations the capacity of the earth to sustain human life has been underestimated; that the earth could support not four times but sixteen times its present population; and that the latter figure could be still further increased by the progress of inventions. But, apart altogether from the accuracy of these figures, the danger of overpopulation is nothing more or less than a myth. Indeed, the end of the world, a philosophic and scientific certitude, is a more imminent event than its overpopulation.

§8. HOW NATIONS HAVE PERISHED

Before speculating on what might happen in the future, it is well to recollect what has happened in the past. The earth has been inhabited for thousands of years, and modern research has revealed the remains of many ancient civilisations that have perished. For example, there were the great nations of Cambodia and of Guatemala. In Crete, about 2000 B.C., there existed a civilisation where women were dressed as are this evening the women of London and Paris. That civilisation perished, and even its language cannot now be deciphered. Why did these civilisations perish? Surely this momentous question should take precedence over barren discussions as to whether there will be sufficient food on the land or in the sea for the inhabitants of the world in 200 years' time. How came it about that these ancient nations did not double their numbers every fifty years and fill up the earth long ago?

The answer is that they were overcome and annihilated by the incidence of one or other of two dangers that threaten every civilisation, including our own. These dangers are certain physical and moral catastrophes, against which there is only one form of natural insurance, namely, a birth-rate that adequately exceeds the death-rate. They help to illustrate further the fallacy of the overpopulation scare.

The following is a general outline of these dangers, and in a later chapter I shall quote an example of how they have operated in the past.

§9. PHYSICAL CATASTROPHES

Deaths from famine, floods, earthquakes, and volcanic eruptions are confined to comparatively small areas, and the two physical catastrophes that may seriously threaten a civilisation may be reduced to endemic disease and war.

(a) Disease

Disease, in the form of malaria, contributed to the fall of ancient Greece and Rome. In the fourteenth century 25,000,000 people, one-quarter of the population of Europe, were exterminated by plague, the "Black Death," and in the sixteenth century smallpox depopulated Spanish America. Although these particular diseases have lost much of their power owing to the progress of medical science, we have no right to assume that disease in general has been conquered by our civilisation, or that a new pestilence may not appear. On the contrary, in 1805, a new disease, spotted fever, appeared in Geneva, and within half a century had become endemic throughout Europe and America. Of this fever during the Great War the late Sir William Osler wrote: "In cerebro-spinal fever we may be witnessing the struggle of a new disease to win a place among the great epidemics of the world." There was a mystery about this disease, because, although unknown in the Arctic Circle, it appeared in temperate climates during the coldest months of the year. As I was able to prove in 1915,[8] it is a disease of civilisation. I found that the causal organism was killed in thirty minutes by a temperature of 62° F. It was thus obvious that infection could never be carried by cold air. But in overcrowded rooms where windows are closed, and the temperature of warm, impure, saturated air was raised by the natural heat of the body to 80° F. or over, the life of the microorganism, expelled from the mouths of infected people during the act of coughing, was prolonged. Infection is thus carried from one person to another by warm currents of moving air, and at the same time resistance against the disease is lowered. Cold air kills the organism, but cold weather favours the disease. In that paradox the ætiology of cerebrospinal fever became as clear as the means of prevention. The story of spotted fever reveals the forces of nature fighting against the disease at every turn, and implacably opposed to its existence, while man alone, of his own will and folly, harbours infection and creates the only conditions under which the malady can appear. For example, during two consecutive winters

---

[8] *Lancet*, 1915, vol. ii, p. 862.

cerebro-spinal fever had appeared in barracks capable of housing 2,000 men. A simple and effective method of ventilation was then introduced. From that day to this not a single case of cerebro-spinal fever has occurred in these barracks, although there have been outbreaks of this disease in the town in which the barracks are situated.

There are many other diseases peculiar to civilisation, and concerning the wherefore and the why an apposite[9] passage occurs in the works of Sir William Gull.

> Causes affecting health and shortening life may be inappreciable in the individual, but sufficiently obvious when their effect is multiplied a thousandfold. If the conditions of society render us liable to many diseases, they in return enable us to establish the general laws of life and health, a knowledge of which soon becomes a distributive blessing. The cure of individual diseases, whilst we leave open the dark fountains from which they spring, is to labour like Sisyphus, and have our work continually returning upon our hands. And, again, there are diseases over which, directly, we have little or no control, as if Providence had set them as signs to direct us to wider fields of inquiry and exertion. Even partial success is often denied, lest we should rest satisfied with it, and forget the *truer and better means* of prevention.[10]

Medical and sanitary science have made great progress in the conquest of enteric fever, diphtheria, scarlet fever, measles, and whooping cough. The mortality from bronchitis and from pulmonary tuberculosis has also been reduced, but nevertheless tuberculosis still claims more victims in the prime of life than any other malady. It is a disease of civilisation and is intimately associated with economic conditions. The history of tuberculosis has yet to be written. On the other hand, deaths from certain other diseases are actually increasing, as witness the following figures from the Reports of the Registrar-General for England and Wales:

---

[9] apposite - apt in the circumstances or in relation to something.
[10] *The New Sydenham Society*, vol. clvi, section viii, p. 12.

Disease	Number of Deaths in 1898	Number of Deaths in 1919
Diseases of the heart and circulatory system	50,492	69,637
Cancer	25,196	41,144
Pneumonia	35,462	38,949
Influenza	10,405	44,801

In view of these figures it is folly to suppose that the final conquest of disease is imminent.

(b) War

War, foreign or civil, is another sword hanging over civilisations, whereby the fruits of a long period of growth may be destroyed in a few years. After the Thirty Years War the recovery of Germany occupied a century and a half. During the fourteen years of the Taiping rebellion in China whole provinces were devastated and millions upon millions of people were killed or died. In spite of the Great War during the past decade, there are some who would delude themselves and others into the vain belief that, without a radical change in international relations and a determined effort to neutralise its causes, there will be no more war; but unless the nations learn through Christianity that justice is higher than self-interest the following brilliant passage by Devas is as true today as when it was written in 1901:

> True that the spread of humanitarianism and cosmopolitanism made many people think, towards the end of the nineteenth century, that bloodshed was at an end. But their hopes were dreams: the visible growth of national rivalry and gigantic armaments can only issue in desperate struggles; while not a few among the nations are troubled with the growth of internal dissensions and accumulations of social hatred that point to bloody catastrophes in the future; and the tremendous means of destruction that modern science puts in our hands offer frightful possibilities of slaughter, murderous anarchical outrages, and rivers of blood shed in pitiless repression.[11]

---

[11] Charles S. Devas, *Political Economy*, 1901, p. 191.

Malthusians may inveigh against wars waged to achieve the expansion of a nation, but so long as international rivalry disregards the moral law their words will neither stop war nor prevent a Malthusian country from falling an easy prey to a stronger people. On the contrary, a low birth-rate, by reducing the potential force available for defence, is actually an incentive to a declaration of war from an envious neighbour, because it means that he will not hesitate so long when attempting to count the cost beforehand. In 1850 the population of France and Germany numbered practically the same, 35,500,000; in 1913 that of France was 39,600,000, that of Germany 67,000,000.[12] The bearing of these facts on the Great War is obvious. In 1919 the new Germany, including Silesia, had a population of just over 60,000,000; whereas, in 1921, France, including Alsace-Lorraine, had a population of 39,200,000. Thus, despite her victory in the war, the population of France is less today than it was seven years ago.

§10. MORAL CATASTROPHES

In view of past history only an ostrich with its head in the sand can profess to believe that there will be no calamities in the future to reduce the population of the earth. And apart from cataclysms of disease or of war, empires have perished by moral catastrophe. A disbelief in God results in selfishness, and in various moral catastrophes. In the terse phrase of Mr. Bernard Shaw, "Voluptuaries prosper and perish."[13] For example, during the second century B.C. the disease of rationalism[14] spread over Greece, and a rapid depopulation of the country began.

The facts were recorded by Polybius,[15] who expressly states that at the time of which he is writing serious pestilences did not

---

[12] *Revue Pratique d'Apologétique*, September 15, 1914.

[13] *Man and Superman*, p. 195.

[14] By rationalism we mean a denial of God and of responsibility for conduct to a Higher Being.

[15] Quoted by W. H. S. Jones, *Malaria and Greek History*, 1909, p. 95.

occur, and that depopulation was caused by the selfishness of the Greeks, who, being addicted to pleasure, either did not marry at all or refused to rear more than one or two children, lest it should be impossible to bring them up in extravagant luxury. This ancient historian also noted that the death of a son in war or by pestilence is a serious matter when there are only one or two sons in a family. Greece fell to the conquering Romans, and they also in course of time were infected with this evil canker. There came a day when over the battlements of Constantinople the blood-red Crescent was unfurled. Later on all Christendom was threatened, and the King of France appealed to the Pope for men and arms to resist the challenge to Europe of the Mohammedan world. The Empire of the Turk spread over the whole of South-Eastern Europe. But once more the evil poison spread, this time into the homes in many parts of Islam, and today the once triumphant foes of Christianity are decaying nations whose dominions are the appanage of Europe. In face of these facts it is sheer madness to assume that all the Great Powers now existing will maintain their population and prove immune from decay. Indeed, the very propaganda against which this Essay is directed is in itself positive proof that the seeds of decay have already been sown within the British Empire. Yet, in an age in which thought and reason are suppressed by systematised confusion and spiritless perplexity, the very simplicity of a truth will operate against its general acceptance.

From the theological point of view, the myth of overpopulation is definitely of anti-Christian growth, because it assumes that, owing to the operation of natural instincts implanted in mankind by the Creator, the only alternative offered to the race is a choice between misery and vice, an alternative utterly incompatible with Divine goodness in the government of the world.

CHAPTER 2
THE FALSE DEDUCTIONS CONCERNING POVERTY

FROM THE ORIGINAL ROOT-FALLACY Malthus argued that poverty, prostitution, war, disease, and a high death-rate are necessary in order to keep down the population: and from the same false premises birth controllers are now arguing that a high birth-rate causes (1) poverty, and (2) a high death-rate. The steps in the argument whereby these amazing conclusions are reached are as follows. Before the death-rate can be lowered the social conditions of the people must be improved; if social conditions are improved there will be an enormous increase of population in geometrical progression; the food supply of the country and even of the world cannot be increased at the same rate; and therefore there will be greater poverty and a higher death-rate unless the birth-rate is lowered. Thus Malthusians argue. In view of the false premises on which their argument is based, it is not surprising to find that their deductions are erroneous and contain many economic and statistical fallacies, to the consideration of which we may now devote our attention.

§1. BIRTH-RATE AND POVERTY

The first false deduction of birth controllers is that a high birth-rate, by intensifying the struggle for existence, increases poverty. In order to bolster up this contention, Malthusians quote three arguments concerning (*a*) famines, (*b*) abundance, and (*c*) wages, and each of these arguments is fallacious.

(a) Famines

The prevalence of famines is quoted as a proof of reckless overpopulation. Now a famine may occur from several different causes, some within and others beyond the control of man, but a failure of crops has never yet been caused by pressure on the soil. On the contrary, famine is less likely to arise in a country whose soil is intensively cultivated, because intensive cultivation means a variety of crops, and therefore less risk of all the crops failing. Moreover, during the past century famine has occurred in Bengal, where population is dense; in Ireland, where population is moderate, and in Eastern Russia, where population is scanty. The existence of famine is therefore no proof that a country is overpopulated, although it may indicate that a country is badly governed or under-developed.

(b) Abundance

Malthusians also claim that by means of artificial birth control we could live in a land of abundance. They point out that, as the population of a new colony increases, the colonists, by applying the methods of civilisation to the rich soil, become more and more prosperous. Eventually there comes a time when capital or labour applied to the soil gives a *maximum* return *per head* of population. Once that point has been reached any further capital or labour applied to the soil will produce a smaller return per head of population. This "law of diminishing returns" may be illustrated by a simpler example. Let us suppose that during one year a market garden worked by one man has produced vegetables to the value of £10. During the second year the garden is worked by ten men and produces vegetables to the value of £200. It is obvious that the work of ten men has produced twice as much per head as the work of one man, because each man has produced not £10 but £20. During the third year the garden is worked by twenty men and yields vegetables to the value of £300. The total yield is greater, but the yield per head is less, because each man has produced not £20 but £15. The point of maximum production per head has been passed, and the law of diminishing returns is operating.

By restricting the birth-rate Malthusians would limit the population to the number necessary for maximum production per head. Now, in the first place, it would be very difficult, if not impossible, in the case of a country with various industries, to decide when the line of maximum production had been passed at any given time. Moreover, it would be utterly impossible to fix this line permanently. In the case of our market garden the introduction of intensive horticulture might mean that maximum production per head required the work of forty men. Again, the very phrase "maximum production per head" implies sterling moral qualities in the workers, and an absence of drones; and sterling moral qualities have never been prominent in any nation, once the practice of artificial birth control has been adopted. Lastly, the Christian ideal requires for its realisation, not a maximum, but an adequate supply of food, clothing, shelter, and fuel. Christianity teaches that to seek after the maximum enjoyment of material things is not the chief end of man, because the life of a man in this world is very short compared with his life in eternity.

(c) Wages

The Wages Fund Theory is an economic reflection of the Malthusian myth. This theory assumes that a definite fixed sum is available every year for distribution as wages amongst labourers, so that the more numerous the labourers the less wages will each one receive. From this theory Malthusians argue that the only remedy for low wages is artificial birth control. They carefully refrain from telling the working classes the other aspect of this Wages Fund theory—namely, that if the workers in one trade receive a rise in wages, a corresponding reduction must be made in the wages of others, so that a rise in wages here and there confers no real benefit on the labouring classes as a whole. That is merely one illustration of capitalist bias in the Malthusian propaganda. In any case, economic science has discarded the Wages Fund Theory as a pure fiction. No fixed or definite sum is available for wages, because the wages of a labourer are derived from the produce of his work. Even in the case of making a railway, where wages are paid before the work is completed, the money is advanced by shareholders on the security of the proceeds that will eventually accrue from the produce of the labourers.

§2. POVERTY IN GREAT BRITAIN DUE TO OTHER CAUSES

(a) Under-development

Even if the theory of birth controllers, that a high birth-rate increases poverty, were as true as it is false, it could not possibly apply to Great Britain or to any other country open to commercial intercourse with the world; because there is no evidence that the supply of food in the world either cannot or will not be increased to meet any actual or possible demand. Within the British Empire alone there was an increase of 75 percent in the production of wheat between 1901 and 1911.[1] In Great Britain there has been not only an increase of population but also an increased consumption of various foods per head of the population. Moreover, if Britain were as well cultivated as is Flanders we could produce all or nearly all our own food.[2]

The truth is that in countries such as England, Belgium, and Bengal, usually cited by Malthusians, as illustrating the misery that results from overpopulation, there is no evidence whatsoever to prove that the population is pressing on the soil. On the contrary, we find ample physical resources sufficient to support the entire population, and we also find evidence of human injustice, incapacity, and corruption sufficient to account for the poverty and misery that exist in these countries. This was especially so in Ireland during the first half of the nineteenth century.[3] Moreover, so far from high birth-rates being the cause

---

[1] Memorandum issued by the Dominions Royal Commission, December 3, 1915 (p. 2).

[2] Prince Kropotkin, *Fields, Factories, and Workshops*, 1899, chapter iii.

[3] Vide *The Economic History of Ireland from the Union to the Famine*, by S. O'Brien (Longmans, 1921).

of poverty, we shall find that poverty is one of the causes of a high birth-rate.

(b) Severance of the Inhabitants from the Soil

It was not a high birth-rate that established organised poverty in England. In the sixteenth century the greater part of the land, including common land belonging to the poor, was seized by the rich. They began by robbing the Catholic Church, and they ended by robbing the people.[4] Once machinery was introduced in the eighteenth century, the total wealth of England was enormously increased; but the vast majority of the people had little share in this increase of wealth that accrued from machinery, because only a small portion of the people possessed capital. More children came, but they came to conditions of poverty and of child-labour in the mills. In countries where more natural and stable social conditions exist, and where there are many small owners of land, large families, so far from being a cause of poverty, are of the greatest assistance to their parents and to themselves. There are means whereby poverty could be reduced, but artificial birth control would only increase the total poverty of the State, and therefore of the individual.

From early down to Tudor times, the majority of the inhabitants of England lived on small holdings. For example, in the fifteenth century there were twenty-one small holdings on a particular area measuring 160 acres. During the sixteenth century the number of holdings on this area had fallen to six, and in the seventeenth century the 160 acres became *one* farm. Occasionally an effort was made to check this process, and by a statute of Elizabeth penalties were enacted against building any cottages "without laying four acres of land thereto." On the other hand, acres upon acres were given to the larger landowners by a series of Acts for the enclosure of common land, whereby many labourers were deprived of their land. From the reign of George I to that of George III *nearly four thousand enclosure bills* were passed. These wrongs have not been righted.

---

[4] William Cobbett, *Social Effects of the Reformation*. Catholic Truth Society (H. 132).

"To urge," wrote Professor Bain, "that there is sufficient poverty and toil in the world without bringing in more to share it than can be provided for, implies either begging the question at issue—a direct imputation that the world is at present very badly managed—or that all persons should take it upon themselves to say how much poverty and toil will exist in any part of the world in the future, or limit the productiveness of any race, because inadequate means of feeding, clothing, or employing them may be adopted in that part of time sometimes called unborn eternity. As a rule, the result usually has been: limit the increase of population without adequate cause, and the reaction causes deterioration or annihilation."[5]

Lastly, there is evidence that poverty has existed in thinly populated countries. Richard Cobden, writing in 1836, of Russia, states:

> The mass of the people are sunk in poverty, ignorance, and barbarism, scarcely rising above a state of nature, and yet it has been estimated that this country contains more than 750,000 square miles of land, of a quality not inferior to the best portions of Germany, and upon which a population of 200,000,000 might find subsistence.[6]

§3. CAUSES OF POVERTY IN INDIA

In reality chronic poverty exists both in the thickly-peopled and in the thinly-peopled regions of India, and therefore the overpopulation theory is an inadequate explanation. Moreover, there are certain obvious and admitted evils, sufficient in themselves to account for the chronic poverty of India, and of these four are quoted by Devas.[7]

(1) The grave discouragement to all rural improvement and in particular to the sinking of deep wells, by the absence outside

---

[5] Quoted by F. P. Atkinson, M.D., in *Edinburgh Medical Journal*, September 1880, p. 229.

[6] Ibid., p. 234.

[7] Charles S. Devas, *Political Economy*, 1901, p. 199.

Bengal of fixity of tenure, the land holder having the prospect of his assessment being raised every fifteen or thirty years. (2) Through most of India the unchecked oppression of usurers, in whose toils many millions of landholders are so bound as to lack means or motive for the proper cultivation of the soil. (3) A system of law and police totally unfit for small cultivators—witness the plague of litigation, appeals as 250 to 1 in England, habitual perjury, manufactured crime, and blackmailing by corrupt native police, all destructive of rural amity, co-operation, and industry. (4) Taxation oppressive both in quantity and quality: demanded, on pain of eviction and imprisonment, to be paid punctually and rigidly in cash, instead of optionally or occasionally in kind, or flexible, according to the variations of the seasons; moreover, levied on salt, raising the price of this necessity of life at least ten times, often much more; when precisely an abundant supply of salt, with the climate and diet of India, is a prime need for men and cattle.

§4. POVERTY IN FACT CAUSES A HIGH BIRTH-RATE

As will be shown in Chapter V, poverty is generally the cause and not the result of a high birth-rate. The Malthusian doctrine has been and is today a barrier to social reform, because it implies that humane legislation, by encouraging population, will of necessity defeat the aim of those who desire to improve the conditions of the poor by methods other than the practice of artificial birth control. To a very great extent Malthusian teaching was responsible for the Poor Law of 1834, the most severe in Europe, the demoralising laxity of the old Poor Law being replaced by degrading severity. Again, as recently as 1899, a Secretary of State reiterated the Malthusian doctrine by explaining that great poverty throughout India was due to the increase of population under the *pax Britannica*. Now the truth is that if the social conditions of the poor were improved, we have every reason to believe that their birth-rate would be reduced, because as civilisation in a community progresses there is a natural decline in fertility. Hence:

(a) Malthusianism is an Attack on the Poor

Both the supporters and the opponents of Malthus are often mistaken in considering his greatest achievement to be a policy of birth control. Malthus did a greater and a more evil thing. He forged a law of nature, namely, *that there is always a limited and insufficient supply of the necessities of life in the world.* From this false law he argued that, as population increases too rapidly, the newcomers cannot hope to find a sufficiency of good things; that the poverty of the masses is not due to conditions created by man, but to a natural law; and that consequently this law cannot be altered by any change in political institutions. This new doctrine was eagerly adopted by the rich, who were thus enabled to argue that Nature intended that the masses should find no room at her feast; and that therefore our system of industrial capitalism was in harmony with the Will of God. Most comforting dogma! Most excellent anodyne[8] for conscience against acceptance of those rights of man that, being ignored, found terrible expression in the French Revolution! Without discussion, without investigation, and without proof, our professors, politicians, leader-writers, and even our well-meaning socialists, have accepted as true the bare falsehood that there is always an insufficient supply of the necessities of life; and today this heresy permeates all our practical politics. In giving this forged law of nature to the rich, Malthus robbed the poor of hope. Such was his crime against humanity. In the words of Thorold Rogers, Malthusianism was part and parcel of "a conspiracy, conceived by the law and carried out by parties interested in its success, to cheat the English workman of his wages, to tie him to the soil, to deprive him of hope, and to degrade him into immediate poverty." When Malthusians enter a slum for the purpose of preaching birth control, it is right that the people should be told what is written on the passports of these strangers.

---

[8] anodyne - not likely to provoke dissent or offense; inoffensive, often deliberately so.

(b) A Hindrance to Reform

The teaching of birth control amongst the poor is in itself a crime, because, apart from the evil practice, the people are asked to believe a lie, namely, that a high birth-rate is the cause of poverty and that by means of birth-control their circumstances will be improved. By one advocate of birth control this weak reasoning and inconsequential sentimentality have actually been crowded into the compass of a single sentence: "We must no longer be content to remain indifferent and idle witnesses of the senseless and unthinking procreating of countless wretched children, whose parents are diseased and vicious."[9] It is true that disease, vice, and wretched children are the saddest products of our industrial system; it is also true that a helpless baby never yet was guilty of expropriating land, of building slums, of underpaying the workers, or of rigging the market. Therefore instead of preventing the birth of children we should set about to rectify the evil conditions which make the lives of children and adults unhappy. Like many other policies advocated on behalf of the poor, birth control is immoral if only on this account, that it distracts attention from the real causes of poverty. In Spain birth control is not practised. I do not say there is no poverty in that country, but there is no poverty that resembles the hopeless grinding poverty of the English poor. For that strange disease, artificial birth control is a worthless remedy; and it were far better that we should turn our attention to the simple words of Cardinal Manning: "There is a natural and divine law, anterior and superior to all human and civil law, by which men have the right to live of the fruits of the soil on which they are born, and in which they are buried."[10]

(c) A Quack Remedy for Poverty

Artificial birth control is one of the many quack remedies advertised for the cure of poverty, and G. K. Chesterton has

---

[9] *British Medical Journal*, July 23, 1921, p. 131.
[10] Quoted in *Tablet*, November 5, 1921, p. 598.

given the final answer to the Malthusian assertion that some form of birth control is essential *because houses are scarce*:

> Consider that simple sentence, and you will see what is the matter with the modern mind. I do not mean the growth of immorality; I mean the genesis of gibbering idiocy. There are ten little boys whom you wish to provide with ten top-hats; and you find there are only eight top-hats. To a simple mind it would seem not impossible to make two more hats; to find out whose business it is to make hats, and induce him to make hats; to agitate against an absurd delay in delivering hats; to punish anybody who has promised hats and failed to provide hats. The modern mind is that which says that if we only cut off the heads of two of the little boys, they will not want hats; and then the hats will exactly go round. The suggestion that heads are rather more important than hats is dismissed as a piece of mystical metaphysics. The assertion that hats were made for heads, and not heads for hats savours of antiquated dogma. The musty text which says that the body is more than raiment; the popular prejudice which would prefer the lives of boys to the mathematical arrangement of hats,—all these things are alike to be ignored. The logic of enlightenment is merciless; and we duly summon the headsman to disguise the deficiencies of the hatter. For it makes very little difference to the logic of the thing, that we are talking of houses and not of hats. ... The fundamental fallacy remains the same; that we are beginning at the wrong end, because we have never troubled to consider at what end to begin.[11]

§5. POVERTY AND CIVILISATION

A modern writer is burdened by many words that carry an erroneous meaning, and one of these is the word "civilisation." Intended to mean "The Art of Living," this word, by wrong usage, now implies that our method of combining mental culture and bodily comfort is the highest, noblest, and best way to live. Yet this implication is by no means certain. On the contrary, the spectacle of our social life would bring tears to eyes undimmed by the industrial traditions of the past hundred years. This I know

---

[11] Quoted from *America*, October 29, 1921, p. 31.

to be true, having once travelled to London in the company of a young girl who came from the Thirteenth Century. She had lived some twelve years on the Low Sierra of Andalusia, where in a small sunlit village she may have vainly imagined our capital to be a city with walls of amethyst and streets of gold, for when the train passed through that district which lies to the south of Waterloo, the child wept. "Look at these houses," she sobbed; "*Dios mio*, they have no view."

CHAPTER 3
HIGH BIRTH-RATES NOT THE CAUSE OF HIGH DEATH-RATES

§1. POVERTY AS NOW EXISTING

THE SECOND CONTENTION of birth controllers is that a high birth-rate, by increasing poverty, causes a high death-rate. In the first place, there is no doubt that poverty, necessary features of which are malnutrition or insufficient food and bad housing, is directly associated with a high death-rate, although this view was once shown by the *Lancet* to need important qualifications.

> With respect to the greater mortality amongst the poor than the rich, we have yet to learn that the only hope of lessening the death-rate lies in diminishing the birth-rate. We have no *proof* as yet that the majority of the evils at present surrounding the poor are necessarily attendant upon poverty. We have yet to see a poor population living in dry, well-drained, well-ventilated houses, properly supplied with pure water and the means of disposal of refuse. And we have yet to become acquainted with a poor population spending their scant earnings entirely, or in a very large proportion, upon the necessities of life; for such is not the case when half the earnings of a family are thrown away to provide adulterated alcoholic drinks for one member of it. Until reforms such as these and others have been carried out, and the poor are able and willing to conform to known physiological laws, it is premature to speak of taking measures to lessen the birth-rate—a proposal, be it said, which makes the humiliating confession of man's defeat in the battle of life.[1]

---

[1] *The Lancet*, 1879, vol. ii, p. 703.

It will be seen that the qualifications practically remove the question from dispute.[2] If the conditions of the poor were thus altered, poverty, as it exists today, would of course disappear. As things are, we find that a high death-rate *is* related to poverty, as is proved, for example, by the death-rate from tuberculosis being four times greater in slums than in the best residential quarters of a city.

The correct answer to the birth controllers is that a high birth-rate is not the cause of a high death-rate, because high birth-rates, as shown in the previous chapter, are not the cause of poverty, but vice versa. Moreover, all the statistical evidence goes to prove that in this matter we are right and that Malthusians are wrong.

§2. HIGH BIRTH-RATE NOT THE CAUSE OF HIGH DEATH-RATE: PROVED FROM STATISTICS

In China, where there is said to be a birth-rate of over 50 per 1,000, and where over 70 percent of infants are helped to die, the high death-rate is due clearly to degraded social customs. In the slums of Great Britain the high death-rate is also due to degraded social conditions. It is not due to the birth-rate. Of this the proof is simple. (*a*) Among the French Canadians, where the average family numbers about nine, this high birth-rate is not associated with a high death-rate, but with the increase of a thrifty, hard-working race. In Ontario the birth-rate went up from 21.10 in 1910 to 24.7 in 1911, and the death-rate *fell* from 14 to 12.6. (*b*) Again, in 1911 the corrected birth-rate for Connaught was 45.3 as against a crude rate of 24.7 for England and Wales; and in

---

[2] Poverty is a term of wide import admitting many degrees according as the victim is deprived more or less completely of the ordinary necessities in the matters of food, clothing, housing, education, and recreation. As used by Malthusians and spoken of here it means persistent lack of one or more of these necessary requisites for decent living. Vide Parkinson, *Primer of Social Science* (1918), pp. 225 sqq.

Connaught, where there is no need for Societies for preventing Parents being Cruel to their Children, the infant mortality rate[3] is very much lower than in England, although the birth-rate is much higher and the poverty much greater. In Bradford, a prosperous English town which pays particular attention to its mothers and children, the infant mortality in 1917 was 132 per 1,000 and the birth-rate 13.2. In Connaught, where there are no maternity centres or other aids to survival, but on the contrary a great dearth of the means of well-being, the infant mortality was only 50, whilst the birth-rate was actually 45![4] So untrue is it to say that a high death-rate is due to a high birth-rate.

§3. A LOW BIRTH-RATE NO GUARANTEE OF A LOW DEATH-RATE

Again, birth controllers claim that a low birth-rate leads to a low infant mortality rate. Now, it is really a very extraordinary thing that, whatever be the statement made by a Malthusian on the subject of birth-control, the very opposite is found to be the truth. During the last quarter of last century a *falling* birth-rate in England was actually accompanied by a *rising* infant mortality rate! During 1918 in Ireland[5] the crude birth-rate was 19.9, with an infant mortality rate of 86, whereas in England and Wales[6] the crude birth-rate was 17.7 with an infant mortality rate of 97, and in the northern boroughs the appalling rate of 120. In England and Wales the lowest infant mortality rate was found to be in the southern rural districts, where the rate was 63, but in

---

[3] The infant mortality rate is the number of deaths of infants under one year old per 1,000 births in the same year.

[4] See Saleeby, *The Factors of Infant Mortality*, edited by Cory Bigger. *Report on the Physical Welfare of Mothers and Children*, vol. iv, Ireland (Carnegie U.K. Trust), 1918.

[5] *Fifty-fifth Annual Report of the Registrar-General for Ireland, containing a General Abstract of the Numbers of Marriages, Births, and Deaths*, 1918, pp. x, xxix, and 24.

[6] *Eighty-first Annual Report of the Registrar-General of Births, Deaths, and Marriages in England and Wales*, 1918, pp. xxiv, xxxii, and xxxv.

Connaught the rate was 50.5. This means that in England a low birth-rate is associated with a high infant mortality rate, whereas in Ireland a high birth-rate is associated with a low infant mortality rate.[7] These cold figures prove that in this matter at least the poorest Irish peasants are richer than the people of England.

§4. VITAL STATISTICS OF FRANCE

The Malthusian claim that a low birth-rate leads to a low death-rate is also disproved by the vital statistics of France.

"The death-rate of France has not declined at the same rate as the birth-rate has, and, while the incidence of mortality in France was equal to that of England in the middle of the seventies, the English mortality is now only five-sevenths of the French. England thus maintains a fair natural increase, although the birth-rate has declined at an even faster pace than has been the case in France. ...

> The French death-rate is higher than is the case with most of her neighbours, and it can quite well be reduced. The reasons for her fairly high mortality are not to be found in climatic conditions, racial characteristics, or other unchangeable elements of nature, nor even in her occupations, since some of the most industrial regions have a low mortality.[8]

I have tabulated certain vital statistics of twenty Departments of France.

The following table, covering two periods of five years in twenty Departments, proves that *the death-rate was lower* in the ten Departments having the highest birth-rate in France than in

---

[7] This is also the emphatic testimony of Sir Arthur Newsholme, in his *Report of Child Mortality*, issued in connection with the *Forty-fifth Annual Report of the Local Government Board* (dated 1917), pp. 77-8.

[8] Knud Stouman, "The Repopulation of France," *International Journal of Public Health*, vol. ii, no. 4, p. 421.

The Ten Departments Having the Lowest Birth-Rate in France

Departments	1909-1913				1915-1919	
	Rates per 1,000 population			Still births per 1,000 births	Rates per 1,000 population	
	Living Births	Deaths	Natural Increase		Births	Deaths
Moselle	27.6	16.5	+11.1	—	14.7	15.4
Finistère	27.2	18.1	+9.1	4.0	15.9	18.2
Pas-de-Calais	26.8	17.4	+9.4	4.2	—	—
Morbihan	25.7	17.8	+7.9	4.4	15.0	19.0
Côtes-du-Nord	24.5	20.6	+3.9	4.2	14.4	20.0
Bas-Rhin	24.3	16.2	+8.0	—	13.3	16.1
Meurthe-et-Moselle	23.2	19.2	+4.0	4.3	—	—
Lozère	22.6	17.3	+5.2	4.2	12.4	17.5
Haut-Rhin	22.4	16.0	+6.4	—	10.3	15.4
Vosges	22.0	18.7	+3.3	4.7	—	—
Total Averages	24.6	17.7	+6.8	4.2	13.7	17.3
The Ten Departments Having the Lowest Birth-Rate in France						
Côte-d'Or	15.4	18.2	-2.8	3.1	9.9	20.5
Allier	15.1	15.7	-0.6	3.3	8.4	18.8
Gironde	15.1	17.3	-2.2	4.5	10.1	21.2
Haute-Garonne	15.1	20.4	-5.3	4.0	9.0	22.5
Lot	15.0	21.0	-6.0	4.5	7.5	20.6
Nièvre	14.9	17.4	-2.5	3.2	8.8	20.0
Tarn-et-Garonne	14.9	20.1	-5.1	4.7	7.9	20.7
Yonne	14.4	19.1	-4.7	3.8	8.9	22.0
Lot-et-Garonne	13.7	19.1	-5.4	4.4	7.4	20.1
Gers	13.2	19.2	-6.0	4.1	6.8	19.8
Total Averages	14.6	18.7	-4.0	3.9	8.4	20.6

the ten Departments having the lowest birth-rate. Moreover, the figures show that, prior to 1914, the Departments with the lowest birth-rate were becoming *depopulated*. On the other hand, the enormous fall in the birth-rate throughout the country from 1915 to 1919 is a memorial, very noble, to the heroism of France in the Great War, and to her 1,175,000 dead. Certain other facts should also be noted. In France the regulations permit that, when a child has died before registration of the birth, this may be recorded as a still-birth; and for that reason the proportion of still-births *appears* higher than in most other countries.

Malthusian claims are thus refuted by the vital statistics of France; but it should be clearly understood that these figures do *not* prove that the reverse of the Malthusian theory is true, namely, that a high birth-rate is the cause of a low death-rate. There is no true correlation between birthrates and death-rates.

§5. COEFFICIENTS OF CORRELATION

As birth controllers rely very much upon statistics, and as figures may very easily mislead the unwary, it is necessary to point out that the Malthusian contention that a high birth-rate is the cause of a high death-rate is not only contrary to reason and to facts, but is also contrary to the very figures which they quote. A high birth-rate is often associated with a high death-rate, but a general or uniform correspondence between birth-rates and death-rates has never been established by modern statistical methods. To these methods brief reference may be made. A coefficient of correlation is a number intended to indicate the degree of similarity between two things, or the extent to which one moves with the other. If this coefficient is unity, or 1, it indicates that the two things are similar in all respects, while if it be zero, or 0, it indicates that there is no resemblance between them. The study of correlation is a first step to the study of causation, because, until we know to what extent two things move together, it is useless to consider whether one causes the movement of the other; but in itself a coefficient of correlation does not necessarily indicate cause or result. Now in this country, between 1838 and 1912 the birth-rate and the death-rate show a correlation of 0.84; but if that period be split into two, the correlation from 1838 to 1876, when the birth-rate was fluctuating, is *minus* 0.12, and in the period after 1876 the correlation is *plus* 0.92. This means that the whole of the positive correlation is due to the falling of the death-rate, and that birth-rates and death-rates do not of necessity move together.[9]

After a careful examination of the vital statistics for France, Knud Stouman concludes as follows:

> In France no clear correlation exists between the birth-rate and the death-rate in the various Departments. The coefficient of correlation between the birth-rate and the general death-rate by Departments (1909-1913) was 0.0692 ± 0.1067, and including Alsace and Lorraine — 0.0212 ± 0.1054, indicating no correlation

---

[9] Dr. Major Greenwood. Vide *The Declining Birth-rate*, 1916, p. 130.

whatsoever. A somewhat different and more interesting table is obtained when the correlation is made with the mortality at each age class:

TABLE II

Under 1 year	0.3647 ± 0.0986
1-19 years	0.4884 ± 0.0816
20-39 years	0.6228 ± 0.0656
40-59 years	0.5028 ± 0.0801
60 years and over	0.2577 ± 0.1001

A peculiar configuration is observed in these coefficients in that a quite pronounced positive correlation exists at the central age group, but disappears with some regularity towards both extremities of life. If the mortality has any influence upon the natality this cannot be in the form of replacement of lost infants and deceased old people, therefore, as has frequently been suggested. That a high death-rate at the child-bearing age should be conducive to increased fertility is absurd, neither does it seem likely that a large number of children should make the parents more liable to diseases which are prevalent at this period of life. The reasons must, then, be looked for in a common factor.

Now the only disease of importance representing the same age-curve as do the correlation coefficients is tuberculosis. This disease causes in France 2 percent of the deaths under one year, 24 percent of the deaths from 1 to 19 years of age, not less than 45 percent from 20 to 39, 18 percent at ages 40 to 59, and less than 2 percent at the ages over 60. Will a high tuberculosis mortality, then, be conducive to great fertility, or do we have to fear that a decrease of the natality will be the result of energetic measures against tuberculosis? Hardly. The death-rate may be reduced, then, without detrimental effects upon the birth-rate.

What can the factor be which influences both the tuberculosis incidence and the birth-rate? We know that the prevalence of tuberculosis is conditioned principally by poverty and ignorance of hygiene, The Parisian statistics, as compiled by Dr. Bertillon and recently by Professor L. Hersch, show a much higher birth-rate in the poor wards than in the richer districts, and the high birth-rates may be furnished largely by the poorer elements of the population. A comfortable degree of wealth does not imply a low birth-rate, as is abundantly shown elsewhere, and one of the important questions which suggest themselves to the French statistician and sociologist is evidently the following: How can the intellectual and economic standard of the masses be raised without detriment to the natality?

We believe that the time is opportune for solving this question. The past half-century has been lived under the shadow of defeat and with a sense of limitations, and of impotence against fate. This nightmare is now thrown off, and, the doors to the world being open and development free, the French people will learn that new initiative has its full recompense and that a living and a useful activity can be found for all the sons and daughters they may get. The habit of home-staying is broken by the war, and new and great undertakings are developing in the ruined north-east as well as in the sunny south.[10]

---

[10] *International Journal of Public Health*, vol. ii, no. 4, p. 423.

CHAPTER 4
HOW RELIGION AFFECTS THE BIRTH-RATE

§1. FRENCH STATISTICS MISINTERPRETED BY MALTHUSIANS

THE FACT that Malthusians are in the habit of citing the birth-rate in certain Catholic countries as a point in favour of their propaganda is only another instance of their maladroit use of figures: because for that argument there is not the slightest justification. The following paragraph from a recent speech[1] in the Anglican Church Congress by Lord Dawson, Physician to the King, is a good example of their methods in controversy:

> Despite the influence and condemnations of the Church, it (artificial birth control) has been practised in France for well over half a century, and in Belgium and other Catholic countries is extending. And if the Roman Catholic Church, with its compact organisation, its power of authority, and its discipline, cannot check this procedure, is it likely that Protestant Churches will be able to do so? For Protestant religions depend for their strength on *the conviction and esteem they establish in the heads and hearts of their people.*

I have italicised the closing words because it would be interesting to know, in passing, whether anyone denies that these human influences also contribute to the strength of the Catholic Church. Among recent converts to the Faith in this country are many Protestant clergymen who may be presumed to have known what claims "on their conviction and esteem" their communion had. Moreover, in France, amongst recent converts

---

[1] *Evening Standard*, October 12, 1921.

are some of the great intellects of that country. If it be not "conviction and esteem" in their "heads and hearts," what other motive, I ask, has induced Huysmans, Barrès, and others to make submission to Rome?

Secondly, it is true that for over half a century the birth-rate of France has been falling, and that to some extent this decline is due to the use of contraceptives; but it is also true that during the past fifty years the Government of France has made a determined but unsuccessful effort to overthrow the Catholic Church; and that it is in so far as the Government has weakened Catholic influence and impeded Catholic teaching that the birth-rate has fallen. The belief of a nation will not influence its destiny unless that belief is reflected in the actions of the citizens. Father Herbert Thurston, S.J.,[2] thus deals with the argument implied:

> Catholicism which is merely Catholicism in name, and which amounts to no more in the supposed believer than a vague purpose of sending for a priest when he is dying, is not likely to have any restraining effect upon the decline of the birth-rate. Further, it is precisely because a really practical Catholicism lays such restrictions upon freedom in this and in other matters, that members of the educated and comfortable classes, the men especially, are prone to emancipate themselves from all religious control with an anti-clerical rancour hardly known in Protestant lands. Had it not been for these defections from her teaching, the Catholic Church, in most countries of mixed religion, would soon become predominant by the mere force of natural fertility. Even as it is, we believe that a country like France owes such small measure of natural increase as she still retains almost entirely to the religious principle of the faithful few. Where the Catholic Church preserves her sway over the hearts of men the maintenance of a vigorous stock is assured.

In the first place, it is noteworthy that the birth-rate varies with practical Catholicism in France, being much higher in those Departments where the Church is more flourishing. As was shown by Professor Meyrick Booth in 1914, there are certain

---

[2] "The Declining Birth-rate" in *The Month*, August 1916, p. 157, reprinted by C.T.S. Price 2d.

districts of France where the birth-rate is *higher* than in the usual English country districts. For example, the birth-rate in Finistère was 27.1, in Pas-de-Calais 26.6, and in Morbihan 25.8. On the other hand, in many Departments the birth-rate was lower than the death-rate. This occurred, for example, in Lot, Haute Garonne, Tarn-et-Garonne, Lot-et-Garonne, and in Gers. In the two last-named Departments the birthrates were 13.6 and 13.0 respectively.

In the following table I have tabulated more recent figures concerning the vital statistics in these two groups of Departments, and rates for the two periods of five years, 1909-1913, and 1915-1919, in each group are compared.

Departments	1909-1913					1915-1919	
	Rates per 1,000 population			Still births per 1,000 births	Deaths Under 1 year Per 1,000 living births	Rates per 1,000 population	
	Living Births	Deaths	Natural Increase			Births	Deaths
Finistère	27.2	18.1	+9.1	4.0	116.7	15.9	18.2
Pas-de-Calais	26.8	17.4	+9.4	4.2	135.3	—	—
Morbihan	25.7	17.8	+7.9	4.4	113.7	15.0	19.0
Total Averages	26.5	17.7	+8.8	4.2	121.9	15.4	18.6
Lot	15.0	21.0	-6.0	4.5	148.0	7.5	20.6
Haute Garonne	15.1	20.4	-5.3	4.0	121.3	9.0	22.5
Tarn-et-Garonne	14.9	20.1	-5.1	4.7	134.7	7.9	20.7
Lot-et-Garonne	13.7	19.1	-5.4	4.4	112.0	7.4	20.1
Gers	13.2	19.2	-6.0	4.1	102.4	6.8	19.8
Total Averages	14.3	19.9	-5.5	4.3	123.6	7.7	20.7

It will be noted that in the three Departments, where practical Catholicism is most flourishing, there is a high birth-rate, and moreover that in these Departments both the death-rate and the infant mortality rate is lower than in the five Departments with the lowest birth-rate.

Professor Meyrick Booth's comments are as follows:

The above five departments (in which the decline of population has been most marked) are adjacent to one another in the fertile valley of the Garonne, one of the wealthiest parts of France; and we may well ask: Why should the birth-rate under such favourable conditions be less than half that which is noted for the bleak district of Finistère? The noted statistician, M. Leroy-Beaulieu, has some interesting observations to offer upon this paradoxical state of things. Considering the country in general, and these districts in particular, he notes that the most prolific parts of France are those in which the people have retained their allegiance to the traditional Church (in the case of the Pas-de-Calais we have a certain degree of adherence to the orthodox faith combined with the presence of a large mining population). M. Leroy-Beaulieu expresses the opinion that the Catholic Church tends, by means of its whole atmosphere, to promote a general increase of population; for, more than other types of Christianity, it condemns egoism, materialism, and inordinate ambition for self or family; and, moreover, it works in the same direction through its uncompromising condemnation of modern Malthusian practices. He draws our attention, further, to the new wave of religious life which has swept over the *baute-bourgeoisie* of France during the last few decades; and he does not hesitate to connect this with the fact that this class is now one of the most prolific (perhaps the most prolific) in the nation. Space forbids my taking up this subject in detail, but it appears from a considerable body of figures which have been collected that, while the average number of children born to each marriage in the English Protestant upper middle class is not more than about 2.0 to 2.5, the number born to each marriage in the corresponding class in France is between 3.0 and 4.0. Taking the foregoing facts into consideration, it would appear that Roman Catholicism—even in France—is very considerably more prolific (where the belief of the people is at all deep) than English Protestantism. This applies both to the upper and lower classes.[3]

In all probability Lord Dawson was unaware of the foregoing, but there is one fact which, as a Neo-Malthusian, he ought to have known, because the omission of this fact in his address is a serious matter. When referring to France as a country

---

[3] "Religious Belief as affecting the Growth of Population," *The Hibbert Journal*, October 1914, p. 144.

where birth control had come to stay, *Lord Dawson did not tell his audience that the Government of France has now suppressed the only Malthusian periodical in that country, and has proposed a law, whereby those who engage in birth control propaganda shall be imprisoned.*

§2. EVIDENCE FROM HOLLAND

As regards other countries, Holland is usually described as the Mecca of Malthusians, being "the only country where Neo-Malthusianism has been given the opportunity of diminishing the excessive birth-rate on eugenic lines, i.e. in the reduction of the fertility of the poorest classes,"[4] and where a "considerable rise in the wages and general prosperity appears to have taken place side by side with an unprecedented increase of population." When we come to investigate this claim we find that, of the eleven provinces of Holland, two are almost entirely Catholic, these being North Brabant, with 649,000 inhabitants, and Limburg, with 358,000 inhabitants. On the other hand, in Friesland, with 366,000 inhabitants, not more than 8 percent are Catholics. The vital statistics for 1913 are quoted by Father Thurston, S.J.:

> ...We find that in Limburg the crude birth-rate is 33.4, in North Brabant it is 32.5, but in Friesland it is 24.3. Of course, this is not the beginning and end of the matter. In North Brabant the death-rate is 16.36, in Limburg it is 15.28, in Friesland it is only 11.21, but the fact remains that in the two Catholic provinces the natural increase is 16.17 and 18.15, while in the non-Catholic province of Friesland it is 13.15. Further, no one can doubt that in such densely populated districts as North and South Holland and Gelderland the Catholics, who number more than 25 percent of the inhabitants, exercise a perceptible influence in raising the birth figures for the whole kingdom. The results would be very different if the entire country adopted Neo-Malthusian principles.[5]

---

[4] The Secretary of the Malthusian League. Vide *The Declining Birth-rate*, 1916, p. 99.

[5] *The Month*, August 1916, p. 157, C.T.S.: 2d.

§3. THE UNITED STATES OF AMERICA

As was proved by the census of religions in 1906, the United States of America is becoming a great stronghold of the Faith. In Massachusetts the Catholic Church numbered 1,100,000 members, whereas the total membership of all the Protestant Churches was 450,000. In Illinois there were about 300,000 Methodists and 1,000,000 Catholics. There were 2,300,000 Catholics in the State of New York, and about 300,000 Methodists, while no other Protestant Church numbered more than 200,000. The New England States, once the home of American Puritanism, are now great centres of Catholicism. Professor Meyrick Booth[6] explains this remarkable change as being due to two causes: (1) The influx of large numbers of European Catholics, who cling tenaciously to their religion; (2) the greater fertility of these stocks as compared with the native population. Moreover, he has tabulated the following statistics:

TABLE IV

State	Population	Chief Religious Bodies (1996).		Births and Deaths (b. and d.)	Birth-rate per 1,000
Indiana	2,700,000	Methodist	233,000	b. 36,500 d. 36,500	13.0
		Episcopalian	102,000		
		Disciples	118,000		
		Roman Catholic	175,000		
Iowa	2,224,000	Methodist	164,000	b. 36,000 d. 20,000	16.0
		Lutheran	117,000		
		Presbyterian	60,000		
		Roman Catholic	207,000		
Maryland	1,295,000	Methodist	137,000	b. 19,000 d. 20,000	15.0
		Episcopalian	35,000		
		Baptist	100,000		
		Roman Catholic	167,000		
California	2,377,000	Roman Catholic	354,000	b. 32,100 d. 32,400	14.0
		Protestants	250,000		
Kentucky	2,290,000	Baptist	312,000	b. 35,000 d. 18,000	15.0
		Methodist	156,000		
		Roman Catholic	166,000		

---

[6] *The Hibbert Journal*, October 1914, p. 147.

In these States the birth-rate is low; in three there are actually more deaths than births; and in all five the proportion of Catholics is comparatively small. These states may be compared with five others, in which the Catholic and the foreign elements are well represented:

TABLE V

State	Population	Chief Religious Bodies (1996).		Births and Deaths (b. and d.)	Birth-rate per 1,000
New York	9,113,000	Roman Catholic Jews Methodist Presbyterian	2,280,000 1,000,000 300,000 160,000	b. 213,000 d. 147,000	22.0
Rhode Island	540,000	Roman Catholic Baptist Episcopalian	160,000 20,000 15,000	b. 13,000 d. 8,000	24.0
Massachusetts	3,366,000	Roman Catholic Congregational Baptist (All Protestants together)	1,080,000 120,000 80,000 450,000	b. 84,000 d. 51,000	25.0
Michigan	2,800,000	Roman Catholic Methodist Lutheran	490,000 128,000 105,000	b. 64,000 d. 36,000	23.0
Connecticut	1,114,000	Roman Catholic Congregational Episcopalian	300,000 66,000 37,000	b. 27,000 d. 17,000	24.0

In these States the birth-rate is very much higher than in the former. Furthermore, a New York paper[7] investigated the birth-rate in that city with special reference to religious belief, and concluded that the different bodies could be graded as follows with respect to the number of children per marriage: (1) Jews, (2) Catholics, (3) Protestants (Orthodox), (4) Protestants (Liberal), and (5) Agnostic. Professor Meyrick Booth, who is himself a Protestant, concludes his survey of the evidence as follows:

> Looking at the situation as a whole, there is good reason to think that the Protestant Anglo-Saxons are not only losing ground *relatively*, but must, at any rate in the East and middle East, be

---

[7] Vide *The Hibbert Journal*, October 1914, p. 149.

suffering an actual decrease on a large scale. For it has been shown by more than one sociologist (see, for example, the statement in *The Family and the Nation*) that no stock can maintain itself with an average of less than about four children per marriage, and from all available data (it has not been found possible to obtain definite figures for most of the Western and Southern States) we must see that the average fertility of each marriage in this section of the American people falls far short of the requisite four children. Judging by all the figures at hand, the modern Anglo-Saxon American, with his high standard of comfort, his intensely individualistic outlook on life, and his intellectual and emancipated but child-refusing wife, is being gradually thrust aside by the upgrowth of new masses of people of simpler tastes and hardier and more natural habits. And, what is of peculiar interest to us, this new population will carry into ascendancy those religious and moral beliefs which have moulded its type of life.

The victory will be, not to those religious beliefs which most closely correspond to certain requirements of the abstract intellect, but to those which give rise, in practice, to a mode of life that is simple, natural, unselfish, and adequately prolific—in other words, to a mode of life that *works*, that is *Lebensfähig*.[8]

As things are, the original Protestant stock of America is being swamped by the growth of the Catholic, the Jewish, and the Negro population. Moreover, the United States is faced by the grave problem of a rapidly increasing coloured race. Despite this fact the American Malthusians are now demanding that a National Bureau should be established to disseminate information regarding contraceptives throughout their country! And what of the other reformers? They also are very busy. They have already abolished those cheering beverages from grapes and grain, or rather they have made alcohol one of the surreptitious privileges of the rich. They are seeking to enforce the Sabbath as a day of absolute rest, not for the glory of God but in order that tired wage-slaves may have their strength renewed for another week of toil in the factories and the mills. Again, they would uproot from the homely earth that pleasant weed whose leaves have made slaves of millions since the days of Sir Walter Raleigh. All these things would they do. There are some things

---

[8] *The Hibbert Journal*, October 1914, p. 150.

the reformers have not done, and these things are recounted by an American writer, Dr. Anthony M. Benedik:

> The divorce peril, the race-suicide evil, the greed for ill-gotten gold, things like these the reformers touch not. And these things it is which harm the soul. Abolishing the use of alcoholic drinks and of tobacco, putting the blue laws into effect, suppressing all rough sports, may make a cleaner, more sanitary, more hygienic, a quieter world. And yet there keep recurring to mind those words of the Master of mankind, 'What doth it profit a man if he gain the world and suffer the loss of his soul?' What worthy exchange can a man make for his soul?[9]

On the other hand, it is good to read that the Governor of New York has recently signed a bill making it a misdemeanour for landlords to refuse to rent apartments to families in which there are children. In that State children thus regain equal rights with dogs, cats, and canaries. Is it too much to ask of the House of Commons that they should pass a similar law? We shall see.

The dangers of birth control were apparent to that great American, Theodore Roosevelt, when he said:

> The greatest of all curses is the curse of sterility, and the severest of all condemnations should be that visited upon wilful sterility. The first essential in any civilisation is that the man and the woman shall be the father and the mother of healthy children, so that the race shall increase and not decrease.[10]

§4. THE SAME RESULTS IN ENGLAND

On a smaller scale the position is the same in England and Wales, where Catholicism has probably checked to some extent the general decline of the birth-rate. In 1919 there were only six towns in England[11] with a birth-rate of over 25 per 1,000, these

---

[9] "Race-suicide and Dr. Bell," *America*, October 29, 1921, p. 31.
[10] *Daily Chronicle*, April 25, 1910.
[11] *Eighty-second Annual Report of the Registrar-General of Births, Deaths, and Marriages in England and Wales*, 1919, p. 89.

being St. Helens (25.6), Gateshead (25.9), South Shields (26.9), Sunderland (27.1), Tynemouth (25.9), and Middlesbrough (26.7). Now in these towns the Catholic element is very strong. During the same year in the four registration counties in which these towns are situated, a larger proportion of marriages were celebrated according to the rites of the Church of Rome than in the other counties of England and Wales.[12] The actual proportion of Catholic marriages per 1,000 of all marriages in these four counties was: Lancashire 116, Durham 99, Northumberland 92, and the North Riding of Yorkshire 92. That gives a fair index of the strength of the Catholic population. Again in 1919 we find that Preston, a textile town, has a birth-rate of 17.1, whereas two other textile towns, Bradford and Halifax, have rates of 13.4 and 13.1 respectively: and there can be little doubt that the relative superiority of Preston is mainly owing to her large Catholic population.

The actual birth-rate amongst Catholics in England may be estimated from information contained in *The Catholic Directory* for 1914. As that work gives the Catholic population and the number of infant baptisms during the previous year in each diocese of Great Britain, and as Catholic children are always baptized soon after birth, it is possible to estimate the birth-rate of the Catholic population. Working on these figures Professor Meyrick Booth[13] has published the following table:

TABLE VI

Diocese	Birth-rate per 1,000 of the Roman Catholic population
Menevia (Wales)	45.2
Middlesbrough	38.0
Leeds	42.0
Liverpool	40.0
Newport	53.0
Northampton	33.0
Plymouth	26.0
Shrewsbury	38.0
Southwark	39.0
Westminster	36.0
Average	38.6

---

[12] Ibid., p. xxvi.
[13] *The Hibbert Journal*, October 1914, p. 141.

During the same period the general birth-rate amongst the whole population of England and Wales was about 24 per 1,000. And figures that are even more remarkable have been published by Mr. W. C. D. Whetham and Mrs. Whetham.[14] These writers, having investigated the number of children in the families of the landed gentry, show that the birth-rate amongst the aristocracy has declined.

"A hundred fertile marriages for each decade from 1831 to 1890 have been taken consecutively from those families who have held their title to nobility for at least two preceding generations, thus excluding the more modern commercial middle-class element in the present Peerage, which can be better dealt with elsewhere. We then get the full effect of hereditary stability and a secure position, and do away with any disturbing influence that might occur from a sudden rise to prosperity."[15]

The results were as follows:

Year	Number of children to each fertile marriage
1831-40	7.1
1841-60	6.1
1871-80	4.36
1881-90	3.13

The birth-rate amongst thirty families of the landed gentry, who were known to be definitely Catholic, was also investigated, with the following results:

Years	Number of children to each fertile marriage
1871-90	3.13

(as compared with 3.74 for the landed families as a whole during the same period)

The interpretation of these figures is not a matter of faith, but of reason. I submit that the facts are *prima facie* evidence that by observance of the moral law, as taught by the Catholic

---

[14] *The Family and the Nation*, 1909, pp. 139, 142.
[15] Quoted in *Universe*, October 22, 1921.

Church, even a highly cultured community is enabled to escape those dangers of over-civilisation that lead to diminished fertility and consequently to national decline.

The truth of this statement has been freely acknowledged by many Anglicans. According to Canon Edward Lyttelton:

> The discipline of the Roman Communion prohibits the artificial prevention of conception, hence Ireland is the only part of the United Kingdom in which the birth-rate has not declined, and the decline is least in places like Liverpool and those districts where Roman Catholics are most numerous.

As we have already seen, there are also other reasons why Catholicism preserves the fertility of a nation.

Without wishing to hurt the feelings of the most sensitive materialist, it is necessary to point out that, apart altogether from the question as to whether the chief or immediate cause of a declining birth-rate is the practice of artificial birth control, or, as seems to be possible, a general lowering of fertility, birth-rates are more dependent on morals and religion than on race and country. During the past century irreligion spread throughout France, and the birth-rate fell from 32.2, during the first decade of the nineteenth century, to 20.6, during the first ten years of the twentieth century. In America, amongst the descendants of the New England Puritans a decay of religion and morals has also been accompanied by a dwindling birth-rate. The decline of the original New England stock in America has been masked to some extent by the high birth-rate amongst the immigrant population; but nevertheless it is apparent in the Census Returns for 1890, when a population of 65,000,000 was expected and only 62,500,000 was returned. Moreover, there is ample evidence in history that, wherever the Christian ideal of a family has been abandoned, a race is neither able to return to the family life of healthy pagan civilisations nor to escape decay. During the past fifty years in England family life has been definitely weakened by increased facilities for divorce amongst the rich, by the discouragement of parental authority amongst the poor, and by the neglect of all religious teaching in the schools. And thus, in the words of Charles Devas, "We have of late years, with perverse ingenuity, been preparing the way for the low birth-rate of irreligion and the high death-rate of civil disorder."[16] The birth-rate in England and Wales reached its highest point, 36.3, in 1876, and has gradually fallen to 18.5 in 1919. During the first two quarters of that year the rate was the lowest yet recorded. During the pre-war year, 1913, the rate was 24.1.

In conclusion, the following statements by a Protestant writer are of interest:

> Judging from a number of figures which cannot be quoted here, owing to considerations of space, it would seem that the English middle-class birth-rate has fallen to the extent of *over 50 percent* during the last forty years; and we have actual figures showing that the well-to-do artisan birth-rate has declined, *in the last thirty years, by 52 percent*! Seeing that the Protestant Churches draw their members mainly from these very classes, we have not far to seek for an explanation of the empty Sunday Schools. ...
>
> Under these circumstances it is not in the least necessary for Protestant ministers and clergymen to cast about them for evidence of Jesuit machinations wherewith to explain the decline of the Protestant Churches in this country! Let them rather look at the empty cradles in the homes of their own congregations![17]

The author of the above-quoted paragraphs thus attributes the decline both of the birth-rate and of the Protestant Churches to the general adoption of artificial birth control. With that explanation I disagree, because it puts the horse behind the cart. When the Protestant faith was strong the birth-rate of this country was as high as that of Catholic lands. The Protestant Churches have now been overshadowed by a rebirth of Rationalism, a growth for which they themselves prepared the soil: and diminished fertility is the natural product of a civilisation tending towards materialism. Although the practice of artificial birth control must obviously contribute towards a falling birth-rate, it is neither the only nor the ultimate cause of

---

[16] Charles S. Devas, *Political Economy*, 2nd edition, 1901, p. 193.

[17] Meyrick Booth, B.Sc., Ph.D., *The Hibbert Journal*, October 1914, pp. 142 and 152.

the decline. The ultimate causes of a falling birth-rate are more complex, and the decline of a community is but the physical expression of a moral change. That is my thesis.

CHAPTER 5
IS THERE A NATURAL LAW REGULATING THE PROPORTION OF BIRTHS AND DEATHS?

§1. THE THEORY OF THOMAS DOUBLEDAY REVIVED

IN 1837 Thomas Doubleday[1] maintained that the rising birth-rate of his own time was closely connected with the fall in the standard of living, and his argument implied that, in order to check the excessive birth-rate, it was necessary to improve the condition of the mass of the people. Four years later he published *The True Law of Population*, wherein he stated that when the existence of a species is endangered—

> A corresponding effort is invariably made by Nature for its preservation and continuance by an increase of fertility, and that this especially takes place whenever such danger arises from a diminution of proper nourishment or food, so that consequently the state of depletion or the deplethoric state is favourable to fertility, and that, on the other hand, the plethoric state, or state of repletion, is unfavourable to fertility in the ratio of the intensity of each state.

By a series of experiments on plants Doubleday discovered that "whatever might be the principle of manure, *an overdose* of it invariably induced sterility in the plant." Although his formula is deficient in that food is selected as the one factor in environment which influences fertility, and although it may be an overstatement to claim that fertility varies in exact proportion to abundance or to scarcity, nevertheless his formula contains an

---

[1] Quoted in *The Law of Births and Deaths*, by Charles Edward Pell, 1921, chap. xii.

important truth which literally knocks the bottom out of the whole Malthusian case.

It is a sad reflection that, while the falsehoods of Malthus have been blindly accepted for the greater part of a century, the work of Doubleday was almost lost in oblivion. His shade has now been recalled to the full centre of the stage, and for this the credit is due to Mr. C. E. Pell. His recent book[2] is a stimulating essay on the declining birth-rate and contains much evidence that supports the main contention of Doubleday. Although it is impossible to agree with all the deductions made by Mr. Pell, he has nevertheless done a public service by restating the problem of the birth-rate in a new way, by effectively bursting the Malthusian bubble, and by tabulating fresh evidence against the birth-controllers.

§2. MR. PELL'S GENERALISATIONS CRITICISED

Mr. Pell defines the law of births and deaths in two generalisations. The first is: "We have seen that it is a necessary condition of the success of the evolutionary scheme that the variation of the inherited potential degree of fertility between species and species must bear an inverse proportion to their capacity for survival."[3] At first glance this statement appears hard to be understood; but it is obviously true—because it means that a species that is well adapted to its environment can survive with a low degree of fertility, whereas a species that is not well adapted to its environment requires a high degree of fertility in order to survive. Mr. Pell considers that a "capacity for survival" is synonymous with "nervous energy"; but, as our total knowledge of nervous energy is limited to the fact that it is neither matter nor any known force, the change in words does not mark a real advance in knowledge.

The second generalisation is that "the variation of the degree of animal fertility in response to the direct action of the

---

[2] *The Law of Births and Deaths*, 1921.
[3] Ibid., p. 40.

environment shall bear an inverse proportion to the variation of the survival capacity under that environment."[4] Here Mr. Pell and I part company. I have already (Chapter 3) disputed the causal connection between birth-rate and death-rate which Mr. Pell here asserts. His generalisation is made by assuming that birth-rates and death-rates rise and fall together that conditions which produce a high death-rate will also produce a high birth-rate and that conditions which cause a low death-rate will also cause a low birth-rate; that the increase or decline of a population is due to the direct action of the environment; and finally that "the actual degree of fertility is decided by the direct action of the environment."[5] On that last rock Mr. Pell's barque sinks. The mistake here is analogous to the old Darwinian fallacy, abandoned by Huxley and by Romanes, that natural selection is a creative cause of new species. Even if the hypothesis of evolution—and it is merely a hypothesis—be accepted, the only view warranted by reason is that variation of species and their actual degree of fertility may be produced, not by the direct action of environment, but by the *reaction* of species to their environment—a very different story.

There is no statistical evidence to prove a uniform correspondence between birth-rates and death-rates, and it is improbable that there should be a physical law of nature whose operations cannot be demonstrated by mathematical proof. Moreover, we know that the same conditions which cause a high birth-rate may cause a low death-rate. In the case of the first settlers in a new country the death-rate is low because the diseases of civilisation are absent and the settlers are usually young, whereas the birth-rate is high. If fifty young married couples settle on the virgin soil of a new country it is probable that for many years an enormous birth-rate, of over 100, will coexist with a low death-rate.

In reality a high birth-rate may coexist with a low death-rate, or with a high death-rate. For example, there is a difference between natural and artificial poverty, the first being brought about by God, or, if any reader prefers to have it so, by Nature,

---

[4] *The Law of Births and Deaths*, 1921, p. 41.
[5] Ibid., p. 40.

and the second being made by man. Under conditions of natural poverty small groups of people in an open country are surrounded by land not yet cultivated: whereas artificial poverty means a population overcrowded and underfed, living in dark tenements or in back-to-back houses, breathing foul air in ill-ventilated rooms seldom lit by the sun, working long hours in gas-lit workshops for a sweated wage, buying the cheapest food in the dearest market, and drugged by bad liquor. In either case their existence is threatened, although for very different reasons, and the birth-rate rises; but under conditions of natural poverty the death-rate is low, whereas in slums the death-rate is high.

§3. THE LAW OF DECLINE

It would appear, then, that under conditions of hardship the birth-rate tends to rise, and that in circumstances of ease the birth-rate tends to fall. If the existence of the inhabitants in a closed country is threatened by scarcity, the birth-rate tends to rise. For example, "In some of the remote parts of the country, Orkney and Shetland, the population remained practically stationary between the years 1801 and 1811, and in the next ten years, still years of great scarcity, it increased 15 percent."[6]

The governing principle may be expressed in the following generalisation. When the existence of a community is threatened by adversity the birthrate tends to rise; but when the existence of a community is threatened by prosperity the birth-rate tends to fall. By adversity I mean war, famine, scarcity, poverty, oppression, an untilled soil, and disease: and by prosperity I mean wealth, luxury, idleness, a diet too rich—especially in flesh meat—and over-civilisation, whereby the physical laws of nature are defied. Now the danger of national decline owing to prosperity can be avoided by a nation that observes the moral law, and this is the most probable explanation of the fact that in Ireland, although the general prosperity of the people has rapidly increased since George Wyndham displaced landlordism over a large area by small ownership, the birth-rate has continued to

---

[6] Dr. John Brownlee, *The Declining Birth-rate*, p. 156.

rise. Moreover, the danger to national existence, as we have already indicated (Chapter 1, §10) is greater from moral than from physical catastrophes, and when both catastrophes are threatened the ultimate issue depends upon which of the two is the greater. Furthermore, it would appear that moral catastrophes inevitably lead to physical catastrophes. This is best illustrated by the fate of ancient Greece.

§4. ILLUSTRATED FROM GREEK HISTORY

The appositeness of this illustration arises from the fact that ancient Greece reached a very high level of material and intellectual civilisation, yet perished owing to moral and physical disasters.

(a) Moral Catastrophe in Ancient Greece

The evidence of the moral catastrophe is to be found in the change that occurred in the Greek character most definitely after the fourth century before Christ. Of this Mr. W. H. S. Jones has given the following account:

> Gradually the Greeks lost their brilliance, which had been as the bright freshness of early youth. This is painfully obvious in their literature, if not in other forms of art. Their initiative vanished; they ceased to create and began to comment. Patriotism, with rare exceptions, became an empty name, for few had the high spirit and energy to translate into action man's duty to the State. Vacillation, indecision, fitful outbursts of unhealthy activity followed by cowardly depression, selfish cruelty, and criminal weakness are characteristic of the public life of Greece from the struggle with Macedonia to the final conquest by the arms of Rome. No one can fail to be struck by the marked difference between the period from Marathon to the Peloponnesian War and the period from Alexander to Mummius. Philosophy also suffered, and became deeply pessimistic even in the hands of its best and noblest exponents. 'Absence of feeling,' 'absence of care'—such were the highest goals of human endeavour.

How far this change was due to other causes is a complicated question. The population may have suffered from foreign admixture during the troubled times that followed the death of Alexander. There were, however, many reasons against the view that these disturbances produced any appreciable difference of race, The presence of vast numbers of slaves, not members of households, but the gangs of toilers whom the increase of commerce brought into the country, pandered to a foolish pride that looked upon many kinds of honourable labour as being shameful and unbecoming to a free man. The very institution that made Greek civilisation possible encouraged idleness, luxury, and still worse vices. Unnatural vice, which in some States seems to have been positively encouraged, was prevalent among the Greeks to an almost incredible extent. It is hard not to believe that much physical harm was caused thereby; of the loss to moral strength and vigour there is no need to speak. The city-state, again, however favourable to the development of public spirit and a sense of responsibility, was doomed to fail in a struggle against the stronger Powers of Macedon and Rome. The growth of the scientific spirit destroyed the old religion. The more intellectual tried to find principles of conduct in philosophy; the ignorant or half-educated, deprived of the strong moral support that always comes from sharing the convictions of those abler and wiser than oneself, fell back upon degrading superstitions. In either case there was a serious loss of that spirit of self-sacrifice and devotion which a vigorous religious faith alone can bestow. Without such a spirit, as history proves conclusively, no nation or people can survive.[7]

(b) The Physical Catastrophe induced by Selfishness

One of the physical catastrophes that probably most accelerated the fall of Greek civilisation was malarial fever. The parasite of this disease is carried from man to man by Anopheline mosquitoes. These insects, during the stage of egg, larva, and nympha, live in water, and afterwards, as developed insects, in the air. The breeding-grounds, where the eggs are laid, are shallow pools of stagnant water. For that reason the disease is most common in marshy country, and tends to disappear when the land is properly drained. Of this we have an example in

---

[7] *Malaria and Greek History*, 1909, pp. 102 et seq.

England, whence malaria disappeared as the marshes were drained.

In Homer there is a disputed reference to malaria, but it is not possible to ascertain whether the disease was present during the rise of Greek civilisation, and there are no references to this disease in the literature from 700 B.C. to 550 B.C.[8] From this date references to malaria gradually become more frequent, and Hippocrates stated that "those who live in low, moist, hot districts, and drink the stagnant water, of necessity suffer from enlarged spleen. They are stunted and ill-shaped, fleshy and dark, bilious rather than phlegmatic. Their nature is to be cowardly and adverse from hardship; but good discipline can improve their character in this respect."[9] After an exhaustive study of the literature, Mr. Jones concludes "that malaria was endemic throughout the greater part of the Greek world by 400 B.C."

Concerning the causes of a malarial epidemic, Sir Ronald Ross writes[10]:

> Suppose that the Anophelines have been present from the first, but that the number of infected immigrants has been few. Then, possibly, some of these people have happened to take up their abode in places where the mosquitoes are rare; others may have recovered quickly; others may not have chanced to possess parasites in suitable stages when they have been bitten. Thus, the probability of their spreading infection would be very small. Or, supposing even that some few new infections have been caused, yet, by our rough calculations in section 12, *unless the mosquitoes are sufficiently numerous* in the locality, the little epidemic may die out after a while—for instance, during the cool season.

The italics are mine, because some writers have suggested that the decline of Greece was *due* to malaria, whereas I submit, as the more logical interpretation of the facts, that a moral catastrophe led to the neglect of agriculture, whereby the area of

---

[8] Ibid., p. 26.
[9] Ibid., p. 85.
[10] Report on the Prevention of Malaria in *Mauritius*, p. 51.

marshy land became more extensive, mosquitoes more numerous, and the fever more prevalent.

In view of the foregoing facts, the following Malthusian statement, although groundless, is nevertheless an amusing example of the errors that arise from lack of a little knowledge:

> The difficulty of providing for a high birth-rate in a settled community was appreciated by the ancient Greeks, notably by Plato and Aristotle; but their conclusions were swept aside by the warlike spirit of Rome, and the sentimentality of Christianity, so that only a few isolated thinkers showed any appreciation of them.[11]

---

[11] C. V. Drysdale, O.B.E., D.Sc., *The Malthusian Doctrine and its Modern Aspects*, p. 3.

CHAPTER 6
THE FALLING BIRTH-RATE IN ENGLAND: ITS CAUSES

BIRTH CONTROLLERS claim that the fall in the English birth-rate, which began to decline in 1876, is mostly due to the use of contraceptives: but the very fact that this claim is made by these reckless propagandists makes it imperative that we should scrutinise the evidence very carefully.

§1. NOT, AS MALTHUSIANS ASSERT, DUE MAINLY TO CONTRACEPTIVES

In support of the Malthusian contention, Dr. C. V. Drysdale, who is not a doctor of medicine but a doctor of science, has published the following statements:

> ... We might note that a recent investigation of the records of the Quakers (the Society of Friends) reveals the fact that family limitation has been adopted by them to a most astonishing extent. Their birthrate [sic] stood at 20 per thousand in 1876 and has now actually fallen to about 8 per thousand. The longevity of Quakers is well known, and the returns of deaths given by their Society show that the great majority live to between seventy and ninety years. Infantile mortality is practically unknown among them, although none of the special steps so dear to most social reformers have been taken for the protection of infant life. The Quakers are well known to be very earnest Christians, and to give the best example of religious morality. Their probity in business and their self-sacrifice in humanitarian work of all kinds are renowned. Yet it would seem that they have adopted family restriction to a greater extent than any other body of people, and, since the decline of their

birth-rate only began in 1876, that it is due to adoption of preventive methods.[1]

Again, he translates the following quotation from a Swiss author:

> In France a national committee has been formed which has as its object an agitation for the increase of the population. Upon this committee these [? there] sit, besides President Poincaré, who, although married, has no children, twenty-four senators and littérateurs, These twenty-five persons, who preach to their fellow citizens by word and pen, have between them nineteen children, or not one child on the average per married couple. Similarly, a Paris journal (*Intransigeant*, August and September, 1908) had the good idea of publishing four hundred and forty-five names of the chief Parisian personalities who are never tired of lending their names in support of opposition to the artificial restriction of families, I give these figures briefly without the names, which have no special interest for us. Anyone interested in the names can consult the paper well known in upper circles. Among them:

176	married couples had	0	children	=	0	children
106	"	"	"	1	child	=	106	"
88	"	"	"	2	children	=	176	"
40	"	"	"	3	"	=	120	"
19	"	"	"	4	"	=	76	"
7	"	"	"	5	"	=	35	"
4	"	"	"	6	"	=	24	"
3	"	"	"	7	"	=	21	"
1	"	"	"	9	"	=	9	"
1	"	"	"	11	"	=	11	"
445	Total					**578**	

That is, an average one and a third children per couple, while each single one of these families could much more easily have supported twenty children than a working-class family a single child.

"Comment on the above is superfluous," adds Dr. C. V. Drysdale, and with that remark most people will cordially

---

[1] *The Small Family System*, pp. 195 and 160, New York, 1917.

disagree. The obvious interpretation of the foregoing figures is that there has been a decline in natural fertility amongst highly educated and civilised people. But that interpretation does not suit Dr. Drysdale's book, and hence we have the disgraceful spectacle of a writer who, in order to bolster up an argument which is rotten from beginning to end, does not hesitate to launch without a particle of evidence a charge of gross hypocrisy against the Quakers of England, a body of men and women who in peace and in war have proved the sincerity of their faith, and against four hundred and seventy respected citizens of Paris. Further comment on *that* is superfluous. At the same time it is obvious that, in so far as their pernicious propaganda spreads and is adopted, Malthusians may claim to contribute to the fall of the birth-rate, and towards the decline of the Empire.

§2. DECLINE IN FERTILITY DUE TO SOME NATURAL LAW

In the course of an inquiry on the fertility of women who had received a college education, the National Birth Rate Commission[2] attempted to discover to what extent birth control was practised amongst the middle and professional classes. Of those amongst whom the inquiry was made 477 gave definite answers, from which it was ascertained that 289, or 60 percent, consciously limited their families, or attempted to do so; and that 188, or 40 percent, made no attempt to limit their families. Amongst those who limited their families 183 stated the means employed, and of these, 105, or 57 percent, practised continence, whilst 78, or 43 percent, used artificial or unnatural methods.

Now comes a most extraordinary fact. Dr. Major Greenwood,[3] a statistician whose methods are beyond question, discovered that there was no real mathematical difference between the number of children in the "limited" families and the number in the unlimited families. In both groups of families the number of children was smaller than the average family in the

---

[2] *The Declining Birth-rate*, p. 323.
[3] *The Declining Birth-rate*, p. 324.

Halliday G. Sutherland

general population, and in both groups there were fewer children than in the families of the preceding generation to which the parents belonged. Dr. Greenwood states that this is *prima facie* evidence that deliberate birth control has produced little effect, and that the lowered fertility is the expression of a natural change. Nevertheless, he holds that the latter explanation cannot be accepted as wholly proved on the evidence, owing to certain defects in the data on which his calculations were based.

> I am of opinion that we should hesitate before adopting that interpretation in view of the cogent indirect evidence afforded by other data that the fall of the birth-rate is differential, and that the differentiation is largely economic. There are at least two considerations which must be borne in mind in connection with these schedules. The first is, that all the marriages described as unlimited may not have been so. I do not suggest that the answers are intentionally false, but it is possible that many may have considered that limitation implied the use of mechanical means; that marriages in which the parties merely abstained from, *or limited the occasions of*, sexual intercourse may have frequently entered as of unrestricted fertility.

The above italics are mine, because, if that surmise be correct, it goes to prove that the restriction of intercourse to certain periods, which restriction the married may lawfully practise, is as efficacious in limiting the size of a family as are those artificial methods of birth control contrary both to natural and to Christian morality. Dr. Major Greenwood continues as follows:

> In the second place, the schedules do not provide us with information as to when limitation was introduced. We are told, for instance, that the size of the family was five and that its number was limited. This may mean *either* that throughout the duration of the marriage preventive measures were adopted from time to time, *or* that *after* five children had been born fertile intercourse was stopped. In the absence of detailed information on this point it is plainly impossible to form an accurate judgment as to the effect of limitation.

There are, therefore, no accurate figures to indicate the extent to which birth control has contributed to the decline in the birth-rate.

§3. AND TO CHARACTER OF OCCUPATION

Moreover, the claim of birth controllers, that the decline in the English birth-rate is mainly due to the use of contraceptives, is rendered highly improbable by the fact that the Registrar-General[4] has shown that in 1911 the birth-rate in different classes varied according to the occupation of the fathers. The figures are these:

	Social Class.	Births per 1,000 married males aged under 55, including retired
1.	Unskilled workmen	213
2.	Intermediate class	158
3.	Skilled workmen	153
4.	Intermediate	132
5.	Upper and middle class	119

Thus, ascending the social scale, we find, in class upon class, that as the annual income increases the number of children in the family diminishes, until we come to the old English nobility of whom, according to Darwin, 19 percent are childless. These last have every reason to wish for heirs to inherit their titles and what land and wealth they possess, and, as their record in war proves them to be no cowards' breed, it would be a monstrous indictment to maintain that their childlessness is mostly due to the use of contraceptives. If *all* these results arose from the practice of birth control, it would imply a crescendo of general national selfishness unparalleled in the history of humanity. No, it is not possible to give Neo-Malthusians credit, even for all the evil they claim to have achieved.

---

[4] *The Declining Birth-rate*, p. 9.

§4. AGGRAVATED DOUBTLESS BY MALTHUSIANISM

Nevertheless, artificial birth control is an evil and too prevalent thing. My contention is that the primary cause of our falling birth-rate is over-civilisation; one of the most evil products of this over-civilisation, whereby simple, natural, and unselfish ideals, based on the assumption that national security depends on the moral and economic strength of family life, have been replaced largely by a complicated, artificial, and luxurious individualism; and that diminished fertility, apart from the practice of artificial birth control, is a result of luxurious individualism. Even if it be so, one of the most evil products of over-civilisation is the use of contraceptives, because this practice, more than any other factor in social life, hastens, directly and indirectly, the fall of a declining birth-rate; and artificial birth control, to the extent to which it is practised, therefore aggravates the consequences of a law of decline already apparent in our midst. I have already said that restriction of intercourse, as held lawful by the Catholic Church, is possibly as efficacious in limiting the size of a family as are artificial methods. If any man shall say that therefore there is no difference between these methods, let him read the fuller explanation given in another connection in Chapter 9. The method which reason and morality alike permit is devoid of all those evils, moral, psychological, and physiological, that follow the use of contraceptives.

CHAPTER 7
THE EVILS OF ARTIFICIAL BIRTH CONTROL

§1. NOT A PHYSICAL BENEFIT

BIRTH CONTROL is alleged to be beneficial for men and women, and these "benefits" are no less amazing than the fallacies on which this practice is advocated. At the Obstetric Section of the Royal Society of Medicine in 1921 the leading physicians on diseases of women condemned the use of contraceptives.[1]

A Cause of Sterility

Dr. R. A. Gibbons, Physician to the Grosvenor Hospital for Women, said that nowadays it was common for a young married woman to ask her medical man for advice as to the best method of preventing conception. The test of relative sterility was the rapidity with which conception takes place. He had made confidential inquiries in 120 marriages. In 100 cases preventive measures had been used at one time or another, and the number of children was well under 2 per marriage. In Paris some time ago the birth-rate was 104 per 1,000 in the poorer quarters and only 34 in a rich quarter of the city; in London comparative figures had been given as 195 and 63 in poor and in rich quarters. These and similar figures showed that women living in comfort and luxury did not want to be bothered with confinements. It had been said that the degree of sterility could be regarded as an index to the morals of a race. Congenital sterility was rare, but the number of children born in England was decreasing. It had been estimated that one-third of the pregnancies in several great

---

[1] *The Lancet*, May 14, 1921, p. 1024.

cities abroad aborted. Dr. Gibbons then quoted figures given by Douglas Wight and Amand Routh to show the high percentage of abortions and stillbirths. In his opinion it was the duty of medical men to point out to the public that physiological laws could not be broken with impunity. It had been observed that if the doe were withheld from the buck at oestral periods atrophy of the ovary took place. In this connection Dr. Gibbons recalled a large number of patients who had used contraceptives in early married life, and subsequently had longed in vain for a child. This applied also to those who had decided, after the first baby, to have no more children, and had subsequently regretted their decision.

Neuroses

Professor McIlroy, of the London School of Medicine for Women, deplored the amount of time spent on attempting to cure sterility when contraceptives were so largely used. The fact that neuroses were largely the result of the use of contraceptives should be made widely known, and also that in women the maternal passion was even stronger, though it might develop later, than sexual passion, and would ultimately demand satisfaction.

Fibroid Tumours

Dr. Arthur E. Giles, Senior Surgeon to the Chelsea Hospital for Women, endorsed Dr. Gibbons's remarks as to the great unhappiness resulting from deliberately childless marriages, and he added that he had always warned patients of this. He believed that quinine had a permanently bad effect. Those who waited for a convenient season to have a child often laid up trouble for themselves. On the question of fibroid tumours he had come to the conclusion that these were not a cause but in a sense a consequence of sterility. Women who were subjected to sexual excitement with no physiological outlet appear to have a tendency to develop fibroids. He would like the opinion to go forth from the section that the use of contraceptives was a bad thing.

All these authorities are agreed that the practice of artificial sterility during early married life is the cause of many women remaining childless, although later on these women wish in vain for children. To meet this difficulty one of the advocates of birth control advises all young couples to make sure of some children before adopting these practices; thus demanding of young parents, at the very time when it is most irksome, that very sacrifice of personal comfort and prosperity to prevent which is the precise object of the vicious practice. Nor is sterility the only penalty. The disease known as neurasthenia arises both in women *and in men* in consequence of these methods. Dr. Mary Sharlieb,[2] after forty years' experience of diseases of women, writes as follows:

> Now, on the surface of things, it would seem as if a knowledge of how to prevent the too rapid increase of a family would be a boon to over-prolific and heavily burdened mothers. There are, however, certain reasons which probably convert the supposed advantage into a very real disadvantage. An experience of well over forty years convinces me that the artificial limitation of the family causes damage to a woman's nervous system. The damage done is likely to show itself in inability to conceive when the restriction voluntarily used is abandoned because the couple desire offspring.
>
> I have for many years asked women who came to me desiring children whether they have ever practised prevention, and they very frequently tell me that they did so during the early days of their married life because they thought that their means were not adequate to the support of a family. Subsequently they found that conception, thwarted at the time that desire was present, fails to occur when it becomes convenient. In such cases, even although examination of the pelvic organ shows nothing abnormal, all one's endeavours to secure conception frequently go unrewarded. Sometimes such a woman is not only sterile, but nervous, and in generally poor health; but the more common occurrence is that she remains fairly well until the time of the change of life, when she frequently suffers more, on the nervous side, than does the woman who has lived a natural married life.

---

[2] *British Medical Journal*, 1921, vol. ii, p. 93.

The late Dr. F. W. Taylor, President of the British Gynæcological Society, wrote as follows in 1904:

> Artificial prevention is an evil and a disgrace. The immorality of it, the degradation of succeeding generations by it, their domination or subjection by strangers who are stronger because they have not given way to it, the curses that must assuredly follow the parents of decadence who started it,—all of this needs to be brought home to the minds of those who have thoughtlessly or ignorantly accepted it, for it is to this undoubtedly that we have to attribute not only the diminishing birthrate, but the diminishing value of our population.
>
> It would be strange indeed if so unnatural a practice, one so destructive of the best life of the nation, should bring no danger or disease in its wake, and I am convinced, after many years of observation, that both sudden danger and chronic disease may be produced by the methods of prevention very generally employed. ... The natural deduction is that the artificial production of modern times, the relatively sterile marriage, is an evil thing, even to the individuals primarily concerned, injurious not only to the race, but to those who accept it.

That was the opinion of a distinguished gynæcologist, who also happened to be a Christian. The reader may protest that the latter fact is entirely irrelevant to my argument, and that the value of a man's observations concerning disease is to be judged by his skill and experience as a physician, and not by his religious beliefs. A most reasonable statement. Unhappily, the Neo-Malthusians think otherwise. They would have us believe that because this man was a Christian his opinion, as a gynæcologist, is worthless. C. V. Drysdale, O.B.E., D.Sc., after quoting Dr. Taylor's views, adds the following foot-note:

"I have since learnt that Dr. Taylor was a very earnest Christian, and the author of several sacred hymns and of a pious work, *The Coming of the Saints*."[3]

Furthermore, in 1905, the South-Western Branch of the British Medical Association passed the following resolution:

---

[3] *The Small Family System*, 2nd edit., p. 2.

"That this Branch is of opinion that the growing use of contraceptives and ecbolics[4] is fraught with great danger both to the individual and to the race.

"That this Branch is of opinion that the advertisements and sale of such appliances and substances, as well as the publication and dissemination of literature relating thereto, should be made a penal offence."[5]

§2. A SCANDALOUS SUGGESTION

The foregoing opinions are very distasteful to Neo-Malthusians, and these people, being unable apparently to give a reasoned answer, do not hesitate to suggest that medical opposition, when not due to religious bias, is certainly due to mercenary motives.

> As the Church has a vested interest in souls, so the medical profession has a vested interest in bodies. Birth is a source of revenue, direct and indirect. It means maternity fees first; it generally presupposes preliminary medical treatment of the expectant mother; and it provides a new human being to be a patient to some member of the profession, humanly certain to have its share of infantile diseases, and likely, if it survives them, to produce children of its own before the final death-bed attendance is reached.[6]

That scandalous suggestion has recently been repeated by the President of the Society for Constructive Birth Control and Racial Progress under the following circumstances. On October 31, 1921, the *Sussex Daily News* published the following paragraph from its London correspondent.

---

[4] ecbolics - an agent that induces contractions of the uterus.
[5] Supplement to *The British Medical Journal*, March 18, 1905, p. 110.
[6] *Common Sense on the Population Question*, by Teresa Billington-Greig, p. 4. Published by the Malthusian League.

Birth Control

Reverberations of Lord Dawson's recent sensational address to the Church Congress on birth control are still being felt as well in medical as in clerical circles. Indeed, the subject has been discussed by the lawyers at Gray's Inn, The London Association of the Medical Women's Federation had so animated a discussion on it that it was decided to continue it at the next meeting. It is quite evident that Lord Dawson did not speak for a united medical profession. Indeed, quite a number of doctors of all creeds are attacking the new Birth Control Society. A London physician has a pamphlet on the subject in the Press, and the controversy rages fiercely in the neighbourhood of 'birth-control' clinics. Much is likely to be made of the example of France, where the revolt against the practices advocated is now in full swing, and strong legal measures have been taken and are in contemplation. French medical opinion is said to be very pronounced on the subject, and it has, of course, a great deal of clinical experience to back it.

On November 8, a second paragraph appeared:

Birth Control

My remark recently that 'a number of doctors of all creeds are attacking the new Birth-Control Society' has been challenged by the hon. secretary of the body in question, who observes that I am misinformed. I must adhere to my statement, which was a record of personal observation. Many doctors have spoken to me on the subject, and their opinions on the ethics of birth control differ widely; but I can only remember one who did not attack this particular society. The secretary suggests that I am confusing what his society advocates with something else. As a matter of fact, the whole question of birth control has been discussed more than once by medical bodies. A doctor who attended one such discussion shortly after the opening of the clinic in Holloway told me that, while there was division of opinion on the general subject, the feeling of the meeting was overwhelming against the particular teaching given at the clinic, as undesirable and actively mischievous. The subject is controversial, and I profess to do no more than record such opinions as are current.

On November 17 the *Sussex Daily News* published the following letter:

Constructive Birth Control

Sir,—Your recent paragraph of 'opinions' about the Mothers' Clinic and the Society for Constructive Birth Control and Racial Progress is not only extremely unrepresentative, but grossly misleading. Your writer says that he can only remember one doctor who did not attack this particular society. This implies that the medical profession is against it, which is absolutely untrue, as is quite evident from the fact that we have three of the most distinguished medical men in Great Britain on our list of Vice-Presidents; four others, also very distinguished, on our Research Committee; and that Dr. E. B.Turner, in a Press interview after the recent Church Congress, singled out Constructive Birth Control as the only Control which was not mischievous.

That there may be medical men who do not approve of birth control is natural, when one remembers that a doctor has to make his living, and can do so more easily when women are ailing with incessant pregnancies than when they maintain themselves in good health by only having children when fitted to do so. Opinions of medicals, therefore, must be sifted. The best doctors are with us; the self-seeking and the biassed may be against us.

Details about the society, including the manifesto signed by a series of the most distinguished persons, can be obtained on application to the Honorary Secretary, at ... London, N.19.—Yours, etc.

Marie C. Stopes,
President, Society for Constructive and Racial Progress.

The italics are mine, and they draw attention to a disgraceful statement concerning the medical profession. As the reader is aware, certain members of our profession approve of artificial birth control. What, I ask, would be the opinion of the general public, and of my friends, if I were so distraught as to suggest that these men approved of birth control because they had a financial interest in the sale of contraceptives? That suggestion would be as reckless and as wicked as the statement made by Dr. Marie C. Stopes. In the *British Medical Journal* of November 26 I quoted, without comment, the above italicised paragraph as her opinion of the medical profession, and on December 10 the following reply from the lady appeared:

Your two correspondents, Dr. Halliday Sutherland and Dr. Binnie Dunlop, by quoting paragraphs without their full context, appear to lend support to views which by implication are, to some extent, detrimental to my own. This method of controversy has never appealed to me, but in the interests of the society with which I am associated, I must be allowed to answer the implications, The paragraph quoted by Dr. Sutherland is not, as would appear from his letter, a simple opinion of mine on the medical profession, but was written in reply to a rather scurrilous paragraph so worded as to lead the public to believe that the medical profession as a whole was against the Society for Constructive Birth Control and Racial Progress. My answer, which appeared not only in the papers quoted but in others, contained the following statement: 'We have three of the most distinguished medical men in Great Britain on our list of Vice-Presidents; four others, also very distinguished, on our Research Committee.' Reading these words before the paragraph your correspondent quotes, and taking all in conjunction with an attack implying that the entire medical profession was against us, it is obvious that the position is rather different from what readers of Dr. Sutherland's letter in your issue of November 26 might suppose.

It will be noted that Dr. Stopes does not withdraw but attempts to justify her scandalous suggestion by stating, firstly, that the full context of her letter was not quoted by me, and secondly, that her original letter was written "in reply to a rather scurrilous paragraph."

As I have now quoted in full her original letter, excepting the address of her society, and the two paragraphs from the *Sussex Daily News*, my readers may form their own judgment on the following points: Is it possible to maintain that the whole context of her original letter puts a different complexion on her remarks concerning the medical profession? Can either of the paragraphs from the *Sussex Daily News* be truthfully described as "rather scurrilous," or are they fair comment on a matter of public interest? Moreover, even if a daily paper *had* published a misleading paragraph about this society, surely that is not a valid reason why its President should make a malignant attack, not on journalists, but on the medical profession?

§3. A CAUSE OF UNHAPPINESS IN MARRIAGE

Nor does birth control lead to happiness in marriage. On the contrary, experience shows that the practice is injurious not only to the bodies but also to the minds of men and women. As no method of contraception is infallible, the wife who allows or adopts it may find herself in the truly horrible position of being secretly or openly suspected of infidelity. Again, when a family has been limited to one or two children and these die, the parents may find themselves solitary and childless in old age; and mothers thus bereaved are often the victims of profound and lasting melancholy. The mother of a large family has her worries, many of them not due to her children, but to the social evils of our time: and yet she is less to be pitied than the woman who is losing her beauty after a fevered life of vanity and self-indulgence, and who has no one to love her, not even a child.

Moreover, these practices have an influence on the relation between husband and wife, on their emotions towards each other and towards the whole sexual nisus[7]. Mr. Bernard Shaw recently stated[8] that when people adopt methods of birth control they are engaging, not in sexual intercourse, but in reciprocal masturbation. That is the plain truth of the matter. Or, from another point of view, it may be said that the man who adopts these practices is simply using his wife as he would use a prostitute, as indeed was said long ago by St. Thomas Aquinas.[9] The excuse offered for illicit sexual intercourse is not usually pleasure, but that the sex impulse is irresistible: and the same argument is used for conjugal union with prevention. In both

---

[7] nisus - a mental or physical effort to attain an end : a perfective urge or endeavor.

[8] *Medico-Legal Society*, July 7, 1921.

[9] *Suppl. Qu.* 49, Art. 6: "*Voluptates meretricias vir in uxore quaerit quando nihil aliud in ea attendit quam quod in meretrice attenderet*" (A husband seeks from his wife harlot pleasures when he asks from her only what he might ask from a harlot). Quoted by the Rev. Vincent McNabb, O.P., *The Catholic Gazette*, September 1921, p. 195.

cases the natural result of union is not desired, and positive means are taken to prevent it.

And what of the results on the mutual love, if an old-fashioned word be not now out of place, and on the self-respect of two people so associated? Birth control cannot make for happiness, because it means that mutual love is at the mercy of an animal instinct, neither satisfied nor denied. It is an old truth that those who seek happiness for itself never find it. And yet the advocates of birth control have the temerity to claim that these practices lead to happiness. I presume that of the bliss following marriage with contraceptives the crowded lists of our divorce courts are an index. The marriage bond is weakened when a common lasting interest in the care of children is replaced by transient sexual excitement. Once pregnancy is abolished there is no natural check on the sexual passions of husband or wife, for they have learnt how sexual desire may be gratified without the pain, publicity, and responsibility of having children. In the experience of the world marriages based merely on passion are seldom happy, and artificial birth control means passion uncontrolled by nature. These methods are not practised by nations such as Ireland and Spain, who accept the moral rule of the natural law expressed in God's commandments and sanctioned by His judgments; and no man who has ever lived in these countries could truthfully maintain that the people there, on whom the burdens of marriage press as elsewhere, are in reality anxious to obtain facilities for divorce. On the other hand, there are many who allege that the people of England are shouting out for greater facilities for divorce than they now possess. At any rate, it is obvious enough that there are those amongst us who are straining every nerve to force such facilities upon them.

§4. AN INSULT TO TRUE WOMANHOOD

It has been said that patriotism is the last refuge of a scoundrel; and apparently chivalry is the last refuge of a fool. Some of the advocates of birth control who have never thought the matter out, either passionately or dispassionately, claim to speak on behalf of women. They protest that "many women of the educated classes revolt against the drudgery, anxieties, inconveniences, disease, and disfigurements which attend the yearly child-bearing advocated by the moralist."[10] What moralist? Who ever said it? Again, they plead for women who "revolt" from the "disfigurement" of the gestation period. The great artist Botticelli did not think this was disfigurement. What true women do? Are they not those of whom Kipling writes, "as pale and as stale as a bone"? And, if so, are these unworthy specimens of their sex worth tears? The vast majority of women bear the discomforts of gestation and the actual perils and pangs of birth with exemplary fortitude: and it is a gross slander for anyone to maintain that a few cowardly and degenerate individuals really represent that devoted sex. But these writers are indeed well out of the ruck of ordinary humanity, because they tell us that "whatever the means employed, and whether righteous or not, the propensity to limit the highest form of life operates silently and steadily amongst the more thoughtful members of all civilised countries," and yet add that "it is not perhaps good taste to consider the means employed to this end." While they thus approve and commend the practice of birth control as natural to "the more thoughtful members," they nevertheless question the "good taste" of discussing the very methods of which they approve, even in the columns of a medical journal! Again, they tell us that "assuredly continence is not, and never will be, the principal" method. That may be possibly true, so long as Christianity is more professed than practised; God knows we are all lacking enough in self-control. And yet throughout the ages moralists have preached the advantages of self-control, and we ordinary men and women know that we could do better, and that others who have gone before us have done better; but it is the self-styled "thoughtful members" who proclaim to the world that self-control in matters of sex is an impossibility, and therefore not to be even attempted. They are no common people—these epicureans, selfish even in their refinement. In addition to losing their morals, they have certainly lost their wits.

---

[10] *British Medical Journal*, 1921, vol. ii, p. 169.

§5. A DEGRADATION OF THE FEMALE SEX

In the Neo-Malthusian propaganda there is yet another fact which should be seized by every married woman, because it is a clear indication of a tendency to reduce women to degrading subjection. No recommendations of limited intercourse or of self-restraint according to the dictates of reason or of affection are to be found in the writings of birth controllers. Unrestrained indulgence, without the risk of consequences, is their motto. To this end they advocate certain contraceptive methods, and the reader should note that these methods require precautions to be taken *solely by the woman*. If she fails to take these precautions, or if the precautions themselves fail, all responsibility for the occurrence of conception rests on her alone; because her Malthusian masters have decided that she alone is to be made responsible for preventing the natural or possible consequences of intercourse. Why? That is a very interesting question, and one to which a leading Neo-Malthusian has given the answer.

In 1854 there was published, *Physical, Sexual and Natural Religion: by a Graduate of Medicine*. In the third edition the title was altered to *The Elements of Social Science*, and the author's pseudonym to *A Doctor of Medicine*. This book, which contains over 600 pages of small type, may be truthfully described as the Bible of Neo-Malthusians, and includes, under the curious heading *Sexual Religion*, a popular account of all venereal and other diseases of sex. In the Preface to the first edition,[11] the anonymous author states: "Had it not been the fear of causing pain to a relation, I should have felt it my duty to put my name to this work; in order that any censure passed upon it should fall upon myself alone." The relation appears to have had a long life, because anonymity was preserved for fifty years, presumably out of respect for his, or her, feelings: and he, or she, must have lived as long as the author, who died in 1904 at the age of seventy-eight; because the author's name was not revealed until a posthumous edition, the thirty-fifth, appeared in 1905, from which we learn that the book was written by the late Dr. George Drysdale, brother of the first President of the Malthusian

---

[11] Reproduced in fourth edition, 1861.

League, and uncle of the present incumbent. The last edition, in recompense for its smudgy type, contains a most welcome announcement by the publisher:

> Publisher's Note.—. . . It is due alike to the reader and the publisher to explain why the present edition is printed (in the main) from stereotypes that have seen fifty years' service. The cost of resetting the work would be prohibitive on the basis of present (and probable future) sales. To some extent the plates have been repaired; but such an expedient can do no more than remove the worse causes of offence.

But the fact with which I am at present concerned is that in every edition all contraceptive methods that apply to the male are condemned for the following reasons:

> The first of these modes [*coitus interruptus*] is physically injurious, and is apt to produce nervous disorder and sexual enfeeblement and congestion, from the sudden interruption it gives to the venereal act, whose *pleasure* moreover it interferes with. The second, namely the sheath, *dulls the enjoyment*, and frequently produces impotence in the man and disgust in both parties; so that it also is injurious (p. 349). ... Any preventive means, to be satisfactory, must be used by the woman, as *it spoils the passion and the impulsiveness* of the venereal act *if the man have to think of them* (p. 350).

The italics are mine, but the following comments are by a woman, who was moreover the first woman to qualify in medicine—the late Dr. Elizabeth Blackwell.

> Here, in this chief teacher of the Neo-Malthusians, the cloven foot is fully revealed. This popular author, who in many parts of his book denounces marriage as the enslavement of men and women, who sneers at continence, and rages at Christianity as a vanishing superstition—all under a special pretence of benevolence and desire for the advancement of the human race, here clearly shows what he is aiming at, and what his doctrines lead to. Male sexual pleasure must not be interfered with, male lust may be indulged in to any extent that pleasure demands, but woman must take the entire responsibility that male indulgence be not

disturbed by any inconvenient claims from paternity. Whatever consequences ensue the woman is to blame, and must bear the whole responsibility.

A doctrine more diabolical in its theory and more destructive in its practical consequences has never been invented. This is the doctrine of Neo-Malthusianism.[12]

§6. SPECIALLY HURTFUL TO THE POOR

(a) Affecting the Young

There are three special and peculiar evils that attend the teaching of birth control amongst the poor. Of the first a doctor has written as follows:

> Morally, the doctrine is indefensible—it follows the line of least resistance, and sacrifices the spirit to the flesh. Materially, it is fraught with grave danger to the home and to our national existence. It is proposed to disseminate a knowledge of contraceptive methods throughout the overcrowded homes of the ill-fed, ill-clad poor. Now it is in these homes that the moral sense has already but little chance of development, where the child of eight or ten already knows far more than is good for the health of either body or mind, and, though we may succeed in reducing the size of the family, yet the means we employ will militate against the raising of the moral tone of the household, and the children will not be any less precocious than before.[13]

That danger is ignored by the advocates of birth-control. "But he that shall scandalise one of these little ones that believe in Me, it were better for him that a mill-stone were hanged about his neck, and that he were drowned in the depth of the sea."[14]

(b) Exposing the Poor to Experiment

---

[12] *Essays in Medical Sociology,* 1899. Revised and reprinted for private circulation, p. 95. (Copy in Library of Royal Society of Medicine.)

[13] *British Medical Journal*, August 20, 1921, p. 302.

[14] St. Matt. xviii. 6.

Secondly, the ordinary decent instincts of the poor are against these practices, and indeed they have used them less than any other class. But, owing to their poverty, lack of learning, and helplessness, the poor are the natural victims of those who seek to make experiments on their fellows. In the midst of a London slum a woman, who is a doctor of German philosophy (Munich), has opened a Birth Control Clinic, where working women are instructed in a method of contraception described by Professor McIlroy as "the most harmful method of which I have had experience."[15] When we remember that millions are being spent by the Ministry of Health and by Local Authorities—on pure milk for necessitous expectant and nursing mothers, on Maternity Clinics to guard the health of mothers before and after childbirth, for the provision of skilled midwives, and on Infant Welfare Centres—all for the single purpose of bringing healthy children into our midst, it is truly amazing that this monstrous campaign of birth control should be tolerated by the Home Secretary. Charles Bradlaugh was condemned to jail for a less serious crime.

(c) Tending towards the Servile State

Thirdly, the policy of birth control opens the way to an extension of the Servile State,[16] because women as well as men could then be placed under conditions of economic slavery. Hitherto, the rule has been that during child-bearing age a woman must be supported by her husband, and the general feeling of the community has been opposed to any conditions likely to force married women on to the industrial market. In her own home a woman works hard, but she is working for the benefit of *her* family and not directly for the benefit of a stranger.

---

[15] *Proceedings of the Medico-Legal Society*, July 7, 1921.

[16] "That arrangement of society in which so considerable a number of the families and individuals are constrained by positive law to labour for the advantage of other families and individuals as to stamp the whole community with the mark of such labour we call The Servile State."—Hilaire Belloc, *The Servile State*, 1912, p. 16.

If, instead of bearing children, women practise birth control, and if children are to be denied to the poor as a privilege of the rich, then it would be very easy to exploit the women of the poorer classes. If women have no young children, why should they be exempt from the economic pressure that is applied to men? And indeed, where birth control is practised women tend more and more to supplant men, especially in ill-paid grades of work. One of the birth controllers has suggested that young couples, who otherwise could not afford to marry, should marry but have no children, and thus continue to work at their respective employments during the day. As the girl would have little time for cooking and other domestic duties, this immoralist is practically subverting the very idea of a home! The English poor have already lost even the meaning of the word "property," and if the birth controllers had their way the meaning of the word "home" would soon follow. The aim of birth control is generally masked by falsehood, but the urging of this policy on the poor points unmistakably to the Servile State. When a nation, or a section of a nation, is oppressed, their birth-rate rises. That is the immutable law of nature as witnessed in history. Thus, the Israelites increased under the oppression of the Pharaohs. Thus, the Irish, from the Union to the Famine, multiplied prodigiously under the oppression of an iniquitous political and land system. By the operation of this law the oppressed grow in numbers, and break their chains.

§7. A MENACE TO THE NATION

(a) There is a Limit to lowering the Death-rate

Birth controllers believe that a high birth-rate is the cause of a high death-rate, and that overpopulation is the cause of poverty. Yet, in spite of their beliefs, they make the following statement: "Neo-Malthusians have not aimed at reducing population, but only at reducing unnecessary death, which injures the community without adding to its numbers."[17] In defence of this statement they argue that if the death-rate falls people will live longer, and therefore the population will not decrease, although the birth-rate is lowered. There are two fallacies in their argument. They overlook the fact that every one of us must die, and that therefore there is a limit beyond which a death-rate cannot possibly fall, whereas there is no limit, except zero, to the possible fall in a birth-rate. If a birth-rate fell to nothing and no children were born, it is obvious that the population would eventually vanish. The second fallacy is that a low birth-rate will permanently lower the death-rate. At first a falling birth-rate increases the proportion of young adults in the population, and, as the death-rate during early adult life is relatively low, the total death-rate tends to fall for a time. Sooner or later there is an increase in the proportion of old people in the population, and, as the death-rate during old age is high, the total death-rate tends to rise. That is now happening in England, and these are the *actual facts* as recorded by the Registrar-General:

> It may be pointed out that, though the effect of the fall in the birth-rate has hitherto been in a sense advantageous in that it has increased the proportions living at the working ages, a tendency to the reversal of this fact has already set in, and may be expected to develop as time goes on. ...
>
> The general characteristics of the figures indicate very clearly the effects of the long-continued decline in the birth-rate of this country, and show, by the example of France, the type of age-distribution which a further continuance of the decline is likely to produce. The present age-distribution of the English population is still favourable to low death-rates, but is becoming less so than it was in 1901. The movements along the curve of the point of maximum heaping up population, referred to on page 61, has shifted this from age 20-25 to a period ten years later, when mortality is appreciably higher.[18]

---

[17] The Secretary of the Malthusian League. Vide *The Declining Birth-rate*, 1916, p. 89.

[18] *Census of England and Wales*, 1911. *General Report, with Appendices*, pp. 62 and 65.

Of these facts the birth controllers would appear to be ignorant. That is a charitable assumption; but, in view of the vital importance of this question their ignorance is culpable.

(b) Birth Control tends to extinguish the Birth-rate

Whatever may be the nebulous aim of birth controllers, the actual results of birth control are quite definite. We have no accurate information regarding the extent to which birth control is practised, for, needless to say, the Malthusians can provide us with no exact figures bearing on this question; but we do know that birth control, when adopted, is mostly practised amongst the better paid artisans and wealthier classes. After full examination of the evidence, the National Birth-rate Commission were unanimously agreed "That the greater incidence of infant mortality upon the less prosperous classes does not reduce their effective fertility to the level of that of the wealthier classes."[19] It is probable that this Commission overestimated the extent to which birth control has contributed to the declining birth-rate; but, even so, this does not alter the obvious fact that artificial birth control, when adopted, reduces fertility to a lower level than Nature intended. If language has any meaning, birth control means a falling birth-rate, and a falling birth-rate means depopulation. Here and there this evil practice may increase the material prosperity of an individual, but it lowers the prosperity of the nation by reducing the number of citizens. Moreover, as birth control is not a prevailing vice amongst semi-civilised peoples, the adoption of this practice by civilised nations means that the proportion of civilised to uncivilised inhabitants of the world will be reduced. If birth control had been extensively practised in the past the colonisation of the British Empire would have been a physical impossibility; and today, in our vast overseas dominions, are great empty spaces whose untilled soil and excellent climate await a population. Is that population to be white, or yellow? A question which today fills the Australian with apprehension.

---

[19] *The Declining Birth-rate*, 1916, p. 37.

(c) A Danger to the Empire

Many people are honestly perplexed by Neo-Malthusian propaganda, and are honestly ignorant of the truth concerning the population and the food supply of the British Empire. They think that *if* the population is increasing faster than the food supply, there is at least one argument in favour of artificial birth control from a practical, although possibly not from an ethical, point of view. They apply to that propaganda the ordinary test of the world, namely, 'Will it work?' rather than that other test which asks, 'Is it right?' The question I would put to people who reason in that way, and they are many, is a very simple one. If it can be proved that Neo-Malthusian propaganda is based on an absolute falsehood, will it not follow that the chief argument in favour of artificial birth control has been destroyed? Let us put this matter to the proof. Neo-Malthusians state that the population of the Empire is increasing more rapidly than the food supply. That is a definite statement. It is either true or false. To discover the truth, it is necessary to refer to the Memorandum of the Dominions Royal Commission, and it may be noted that publications of that sort are not usually read by the general public to whom the Neo-Malthusians appeal. The public are aware that the staff of life is made from wheat, but they are not aware of the following facts, which prove that in this matter, at any rate, Neo-Malthusian statements are absolutely false. In foreign countries the increase of the wheat area is proceeding at practically the same rate as the increase of population. Within the British Empire *the wheat area is increasing more rapidly than the population.* Between 1901 and 1911 the percentage increase of the wheat area *was nearly seven times greater* than the increase of population; and the percentage increase in the actual production of wheat *was nearly twelve times greater* than the increase of population. As these facts alone completely refute the Neo-Malthusian argument, it is advisable to reproduce here the official statistics.[20]

---

[20] Dominions Royal Commission, Memorandum and Tables relating to the Food and Raw Material Requirements of the United Kingdom: prepared by the Royal Commission on the Natural

The requirements of wheat[21] for the United Kingdom and the extent to which Home and overseas supplies contributed towards these requirements during the period under review can be briefly summarised by the following table, viz.:

Annual average	Normal requirements	Supplies		Proportion of Supply	
		Home	Overseas	Home	Overseas
	Million cwts.	Million cwts.	Million cwts.	%	%
1901-5	138.8	28.7	110.1	20.7	79.3
1906-10	143.2	31.9	111.3	22.3	77.7
1911-13	149.2	32.9	116.3	22.1	77.9

The main sources of overseas supply are too well known to require recapitulation here. The imports from the Dominions and India and their proportionate contribution to the United Kingdom's total imports and wheat requirements since 1901 have been as follows:

From	1901-5			1906-10			1911-13		
	Annual Avg*.	Total imports	Total Require-ments	Annual Avg.*	Total imports	Total Require-ments	Annual Avg.*	Total imports	Total Require-ments
Canada	10.3	9.2%	7.4%	17.2	15.1%	12.0%	24.5	20.5%	16.4%
Australia	6.6	5.9%	4.8%	9.4	8.2%	6.6%	12.6	10.6%	8.4%
New Zealand	0.4	0.4%	0.3%	0.3	0.3%	0.2%	0.4	0.3%	0.3%
India	15.5	13.9%	11.2%	13.3	11.7%	9.3%	21.5	18.0%	14.4%
	32.8	29.4%	23.7%	40.2	35.3%	28.1%	59.0	49.4%	39.5%

*In million Hundredweights, which is a unit of measurement for weight used in certain commodities trading contracts such as livestock and grains.

The large increase in the proportion received from the Dominions is, of course, mainly due to the great extension of wheat cultivation in Western Canada since the beginning of the century.[22]

Future Supplies

As the United Kingdom is dependent for so large a proportion of its wheat supplies on the surplus of oversea countries, it is of

---

Resources, Trade, and Legislation of Certain Portions of His Majesty's Dominions. November 1915, pp. 1 and 2. My italics.—H. G. S.

[21] i.e. grain, wheatmeal, and flour.

[22] For particulars of this increase see Canada Year Book 1913, p. 144.

material interest to examine whether this surplus is increasing, or whether the growth of population is proceeding more rapidly than the extension of the wheat-growing area.

The Board of Agriculture and Fisheries in 1912 estimated[23] that the extension of the wheat area and the growth of population during the period 1901-1911 was as follows:

Wheat-growing countries	Wheat area**		% increase	Population***		% increase
	1901	1911		1901	1911	
British Empire*	34,696	50,490	+45.5	283,385	302,154	+6.6
European countries	98,326	115,105	+17.1	291,685	337,181	+15.6
Others	34,696	50,490	+45.5	283,385	302,154	+6.6

*Includes United Kingdom, Canada, Australia, New Zealand, and India.
** In thousand acres.
*** In thousands.

It is important to find that, while in foreign countries, both European and extra-European, the increase of wheat area is proceeding at practically the same rate as the increase of population, in the British Empire the wheat area is developing far more rapidly, so that the Empire as a whole is becoming more self-supporting.

The total production of wheat within the British Empire, which was 227,500,000 cwts. in 1901, had risen to 399,700,000 cwts. in 1911, an increase of 75 percent.

The relative yield per acre in 1911 was as follows:

	Yield per acre (Bushels)	
	Average of 1906-10	1911
United Kingdom	32.77	32.96
Canada	17.56[24]	20.80[25]
Australia	11.74	9.65[26]
New Zealand	28.72	36.73
India (including Native States)	11.44	12.02

[23] See pp. 387-8 of [Cd. 6588].

[24] Average for period 1907-1910 and excluding British Columbia, where the yield per acre in 1911, the only year for which figures are available, averaged 29.37 bushels.

[25] Including British Columbia.

[26] Below the average. The yield per acre in 1912 was 12.53 bushels, and in 1913 11.18.

The foregoing facts destroy the chief Neo-Malthusian argument, and, as birth control tends to extinguish the birth-rate, this Neo-Malthusian propaganda is a menace to the Empire. In fact, the danger is very great for the simple reason that the proportion of white people within the Empire is very small.

The British Empire's share of the world's people is very large, but it mainly consists, it should be remembered, of Asiatics and African natives. The Empire as a whole contains about 450 millions of the world's 1,800 millions, made up roundly as follows:

United Kingdom: 47,000,000
Self-governing Dominions: 22,000,000
Rest of the Empire[27]: 378,000,000
Total: 447,000,000

Of the great aggregate Empire population of 447 millions, the white people account for no more than 65 millions. That is to say, outside the United Kingdom itself the Empire has only 18 million white people, or less than four million families. That figure, of course, includes Boers, French-Canadians, and others of foreign extraction. This fact is clearly not realised by those present-day Malthusians who assure us that too many Britons are being born.[28]

It is also well to remember that depopulation in Italy preceded the disintegration of the Roman Empire. Historians have estimated that, while under the Republic, Italy could raise an army of 800,000 men, under Titus that number was halved.

Unfortunately, there are some to whom this argument will not appeal, and wandering about in our midst are a few lost souls, so bemused by the doctrines of international finance that they see no virtue in patriotism or, in other words, in the love that a man has for his own home. They are unmoved by the story of sacrifice, of thrift, and of patient trust in God that is told for instance in the history of the Protestant manses of Scotland, where ministers on slender stipends brought up families of ten

---

[27] Chiefly India, 319 millions
[28] *The Observer*, Nov. 11, 1921.

and twelve, where the boys won scholarships at the universities, and where women were the mothers of men.

These days have been recalled by Norman Macleod:

> The minister, like most of his brethren, soon took to himself a wife, the daughter of a neighbouring 'gentleman tacksman,' and the grand-daughter of a minister, well born and well bred; and never did man find a help more meet for him. In that manse they lived for nearly fifty years, and there were born to them sixteen children; yet neither father nor mother could ever lay hand on a child and say, 'We wish this one had not been.' They were all a source of unmingled joy. ...[29]
>
> A 'wise' neighbour once remarked, 'That minister with his large family will ruin himself, and if he dies they will be beggars.' Yet there has never been a beggar among them to the fourth generation.[30]

How did they manage to provide for their children? In this pagan, spoon-fed age, many people will laugh when they read the answer—in a family letter, written more than a hundred years ago by a man who was poor:

> But the thought—I cannot provide for these! Take care, minister, the anxiety of your affection does not unhinge that confidence with which the Christian ought to repose upon the wise and good providence of God! What though you are to leave your children poor and friendless? Is the arm of the Lord shortened, that He cannot help? Is His ear heavy, that He cannot hear? You yourself have been no more than an instrument in the hand of His goodness; and is His goodness, pray, bound up in your feeble arm? Do you what you can; leave the rest to God. Let them be good, and fear the Lord, and keep His commandments, and He will provide for them in His own way and in His own time. Why, then, wilt thou be cast down, O my soul; why disquieted within me? Trust thou in the Lord! Under all the changes and the cares and the troubles of this life, may the consolations of religion support our spirits. In the multitude of the thoughts within me, Thy comforts O my God, delight my soul! But no more of this preaching-like

---

[29] *Reminiscences of a Highland Parish*, by Norman Macleod, D.D., 1876, p. 27

[30] Ibid., p. 34.

harangue, of which, I doubt not, you wish to be relieved. Let me rather reply to your letter, and tell you my news.[31]

That letter was written by Norman Macleod, ordained in 1774, and minister of the Church of Scotland in Morven for some forty years. His stipend was £40, afterwards raised to £80. He had a family of sixteen. One of his sons was minister in Campbelltown, and later in Glasgow. He had a family of eleven. His eldest son was Chaplain to Queen Victoria and wrote the *Reminiscences of a Highland Parish*.

The birth controllers ask why we should bring up children at great cost and trouble to ourselves, and they have been well answered by a non-Catholic writer, Dr. W. E. Home.[32]

> One of my acquaintances refuses to have a second child because he could not then play golf. Is there, then, no pleasure in children which shall compensate for the troubles and expenses they bring upon you? I notice that the penurious Roman Catholic French Canadian farmers are spreading out of Quebec and occupying more and more of Ontario. I fancy these hard-living parents would think their struggles to bring up their large (ten to twenty) families worthwhile when they see how their group is strengthening its position. If a race comes to find no instinctive pleasure in children it will probably be swept away by others more virile. One man will live where another will starve; prudence and selfishness are not identical.
>
> In her book, *The Strength of a People*, Mrs. Bosanquet, who signed the Majority Report of the Poor Law Commission, tells the story of two girls in domestic service who became engaged. One was imprudent, married at once, lived in lodgings, trusted to the Church and the parish doctor to see her through her first confinement, had no foresight or management, every succeeding child only added to her worries, and her marriage was a failure. The other was prudent, did not marry till, after six months, she and her fiancé had chosen a house and its furniture. Then she married, and their house was their own careful choice; every table and chair reminded them of the afternoon they had had together when it was chosen; they were amusement enough to themselves, and they

---

[31] Ibid., p. 91.
[32] *British Medical Journal*, August 13, 1921, p. 261.

saved their money for the expenses of her confinement. He had not to seek amusement outside his home, did his work with a high sanction and got promoted, and each child was only an added pleasure. Idyllic; yes, but sometimes true. One of the happiest men I have known was a Marine sergeant with ten children, and a bed in his house for stray boys he thought he should help.

One of my friends married young and had five children; this required management. He certainly could not go trips, take courses and extra qualifications, but he did his work all right, and his sons were there to help in the war, and one of them has won a position of Imperial usefulness far above that of his father or me. Is that no compensation to his parents for old-time difficulties they have by now almost forgotten? A bad tree cannot bring forth good fruit.

Dr. W. E. Home is right, and the Neo-Malthusian golfer is wrong. Moreover, he is wrong as a golfer. Golf requires skill, a fine coordination of sight and touch, much patience and self-control: and many unfortunate people lack these qualities of mind and body and are therefore unable to play this game with pleasure to themselves or to others. Consequently, every golfer, no matter whether he accepts the hypothesis of Spencer or that of Weismann concerning the inheritance of acquired characteristics, should rejoice to see his large family in the links as a good omen for the future of this game, although there be some other reasons that also justify the existence of children.

(d) The Dangers of Small Families

In a Malthusian leaflet, written for the poor Dr. Binnie Dunlop states:

> You must at least admit that there would be nothing like the usual poverty if married couples had only one child for every 20s. or so, a week of wages. Yet the population would continue to increase rapidly, because very few of the children of small families die or grow up weakly; and it would become stronger, richer, and of course much happier.[33]

---

[33] Leaflet of the Malthusian League.

The false suggestion contained in his first sentence, namely that a high birth-rate is the cause of poverty, has already been exposed (Chap. 2), and apparently Dr. Binnie Dunlop has never considered *why* so many of the English people should be so poor as to enable him to make use of their very poverty in order to tempt them to adopt an evil method of birth control. Moreover, his second contention, that a small family produces a higher type of child, better fed, better trained, and healthier, than is found amongst the children of large families is contrary to the following facts, as stated by Professor Meyrick Booth:

> 1. A civilisation cannot be maintained with an average of less than about four children per marriage; a smaller number will lead to actual extinction.
> 2. Much information exists tending to show that heredity strongly favours the third, fourth, fifth, and subsequent children born to a given couple, rather than the first two, who are peculiarly apt to inherit some of the commonest physical and mental defects (upon this important point the records of the University of London Eugenics Laboratory should be consulted). A population with a low birth-rate thus naturally tends to degenerate. *It is the normal, and not the small family, that gives the best children.*
> 3. The present differential birth-rate—high amongst the less intelligent classes and low amongst the most capable families—so far from leading upwards, is causing the race to breed to a lower type.
> 4. The small family encourages the growth of luxury and the development of what M. Leroy-Beaulieu calls *l'esprit arriviste*.
> 5. The popular idea that *childbirth is injurious* to a woman's health is probably *quite erroneous*. Where the *birth-rate is high the health of the woman is apparently better* than where it is artificially low.
> 6. A study of history does not show that nations with low birth-rates have been able to attain to a higher level of civilisation. Such nations have been thrust into the background by their hardier neighbours.[34]

---

[34] *The Hibbert Journal*, October 1914, p. 153. My italics.—H. G. S.

Moreover, M. Leroy-Beaulieu, in *La Question de la Population*,[35] states that those districts of France which show an exceptionally low birth-rate are distinguished by a peculiar atmosphere of materialism, and that their inhabitants exhibit, in a high degree, an attitude of mind well named *l'esprit arriviste*—the desire to concentrate on outward success, to push on, to be climbers, to advance themselves and their children in fashionable society. This spirit means the willing sacrifice of all ideals of ethics or of patriotism to family egoism. To this mental attitude, and to the corresponding absence of religion, he attributes the decline of population. In conclusion the following evidence is quoted by Professor Meyrick Booth:

> The *Revue des Deux Mondes* for July 1911 contains a valuable account, by a doctor resident in Gascony, of the state of things in that part of France (where, it will be remembered, the birth-rate is especially low). He expresses with the utmost emphasis the conviction that the Gascons are deteriorating, physically and mentally, and points out, at the same time, that the decline of population has had an injurious effect upon the economic condition of the country. *L'hyponatalité est une cause précise et directe de la dégénérescence de la race*, he writes. And, dealing with the belief that a low birthrate will result in the development of a superior type of child, he says: *C'est une illusion qui ne résiste pas à la lumière des faits tels que les montre l'étude démographique de nos villages gascons. Depuis que beaucoup de bancs restent vides à la petite école, les écoliers ne sont ni mieux doués, ni plus travailleurs, et ils sont certainement moins vigoureux.* And again, *La quantité est en général la condition première et souveraine de la qualité.*[36]

§8. THE PLOT AGAINST CHRISTENDOM

All purposive actions are ultimately based on philosophy of one sort or another. If, for example, we find a rich man founding hospitals for the poor, we may assume that he believes in the

---

[35] Quoted by Professor Meyrick Booth, *The Hibbert Journal*, October 1914, p. 153.

[36] *The Hibbert Journal*, October 1914.

principle of Charity. It is, therefore, of prime importance to determine what kind of philosophy underlies Neo-Malthusian propaganda. The birth controllers profess to be actuated solely by feelings of compassion and of benevolence towards suffering humanity; and it is on these grounds that they are appealing to the Church of England to bless their work, or at least to lend to their propaganda a cloak of respectability. Now, the very fact that Neo-Malthusians are sincere in their mistaken and dangerous convictions makes it all the more necessary that we should discover the doctrines on which their propaganda was originally based; because, although their economic fallacies were borrowed from Malthus, their philosophy came from a different source.

This philosophy is to be found, naked and unashamed, in a book entitled *The Elements of Social Science*. I have already referred to this work as the Bible of Neo-Malthusians, and its teaching has been endorsed as recently as 1905 by the official journal of the Malthusian League, as witness the following eulogy, whose last lines recall the happy days of Bret Harte in the Far West, and the eloquent periods of our old and valued friend Colonel Starbottle:

> This work should be read by all followers of J. S. Mill, Garnier, and the Neo-Malthusian school of economists. We could give a long criticism of the many important chapters in this book; but, as we might be considered as prejudiced in its favour because of our agreement with its aims, we prefer to cite the opinion given by the editor of that widely circulated and most enlightened paper *The Weekly Times and Echo*, which appears in its issue of October 8.[37]

Before quoting from the book an explanation is due to my readers. I do not suggest that all of those who are today supporting the propaganda for artificial birth control would agree with its foolish blasphemies and drivelling imbecilities; but it is nevertheless necessary to quote these things, because our birth controllers are too wise in their day and generation to reveal to the public, still less to the Church of England, *the philosophy*

---

[37] *The Malthusian*, November 1905, p. 84.

on which Neo-Malthusianism was originally based, and from which it has grown. Moreover, the Malthusians claim that it was the author of the *Elements of Social Science* "who interested Mr. Charles Bradlaugh and Mrs. Annie Besant in the question."[38] Four quotations from the last edition of the book will suffice:

> But this is a certain truth, that any human being, any one of us, no matter how fallen and degraded, is an infinitely more glorious and adorable being than any God that ever was or will be conceived (p. 413).

In justice to the memory of John Stuart Mill, whom Malthusians are ever quoting, it should be noted that the foregoing blasphemy is nothing more nor less than a burlesque of Positivism or of Agnosticism. The teaching of Mill, Bain, and of Herbert Spencer was that the knowledge of God and of His nature is impossible, because our senses are the only source of knowledge. Their reasoning was wrong—because a primary condition of all knowledge is memory, in itself an intuition, because primary mathematical axioms are intellectual intuitions, and because mind has the power of abstraction; but, even so, not one of these men was capable of having written the above-quoted passage. The next quotation refers to marriage.

> Marriage is based upon the idea that constant and unvarying love is the only one which is pure and honourable, and which should be recognised as morally good. But there could not be a greater error than this. Love is, like all other human passions and appetites, subject to change, deriving a great part of its force and continuance from variety in its objects; and to attempt to fix it to an invariable channel is to try to alter the laws of its nature (p. 353).

That quotation is an example of how evil ideas may arise from muddled thinking: because if the word "lust" be substituted for the word "love" in the third sentence, the remaining forty-

---

[38] C. V. Drysdale, O.B.E., D.Sc., *The Small Family System*, 1918, p. 150.

five words would merely convey a simple truth, expressed by Kipling in two lines:
"For the more you 'ave known o' the others
The less will you settle to one."

Very few people, I suppose, are so foolish as to believe that man is by nature either a chaste or a constant animal, and indeed in this respect he appears to his disadvantage when compared with certain varieties of birds, which are *by nature* constant to each other. On the other hand, millions of people believe that man is able to overcome his animal nature; and for the past two thousand years the civilised races of the world have held that this is a goal towards which mankind should strive. In the opinion of Christendom chastity and marriage are both morally good, but, according to the philosophy of our Neo-Malthusian author, they are morally evil.

> Chastity, or complete sexual abstinence, so far from being a virtue, is invariably a great natural sin (p. 162).

Is it not obvious that to the writers of such passages love is synonymous with animalism, with lust? It is by no means necessary to go to saints or to moralists for a refutation of this Neo-Malthusian philosophy. Does any decent ordinary man or woman agree with it? Ask the man in the street. Turn the pages of our literature. Refer to Chaucer or Spenser, to Shakespeare or Milton, refer to Fielding or Burns or Scott or Tennyson. Some of these men were very imperfect; but they all knew the difference between lust and love; and it is because they can tell us at least something of that which is precious, enduring, ethereal, and divine in love that we read their pages and honour their names. Not one of these men could have written the following sentence:

> Marriage distracts our attention from the real sexual duties, and this is one of its worst effects (p.366).

Now it is certain that if "the real sexual duties" are represented by promiscuous fornication, then both marriage and chastity are evil things. That philosophy is very old. From time immemorial it has been advocated by one of the most powerful intelligences in the universe. Such is the soil on which the Neo-Malthusian fungus has grown—a soil that would rot the foundations of Europe.

CHAPTER 8
THE RELIGIOUS ARGUMENT AGAINST BIRTH CONTROL

§1. AN OFFENCE AGAINST THE LAW OF NATURE

BIRTH CONTROL is against the law of nature, which Christians believe to be the reflection of the divine law in human affairs, and any violation of this law was held to be vicious even by the ancient pagan world. To this argument an advocate of birth control has made answer:

> We interfere with nature at every point—we shave, cut our hair, cook our food, fill cavities in our teeth (or wear artificial teeth), clothe ourselves, wear boots, hats, and wash our faces, so why should birth alone be sacred from the touch and play of human moulding?[1]

Why? For a very simple reason. Birth control belongs to the moral sphere; it essentially affects man's progress in good, whereas all the other things that he mentions have no more moral significance than has the practice of agriculture. Regarded in the light of the law of nature they are neutral actions, neither good nor bad in themselves, raising no question of right or wrong, and having no real bearing on the accomplishment of human destiny. To make no distinction between the merely physical law of nature (expressed in the invariable tendency of everything to act according to its kind) and the natural moral law which governs human conduct, is to pronounce oneself a materialist. Yet even a materialist ought to denounce the practice of birth control, as it violates the laws of nature which regulate physical well-being.

---

[1] *British Medical Journal*, August 6, 1927, p. 219.

"But," says the materialist, "it is not possible for anyone to act against nature, because all actions take place *in* nature, and therefore every act is a natural act." Quite so: in that sense murder is a natural act; even unnatural vice is a natural act. Will any one defend them? There is a natural law in the physical world, and there is a natural law in conscience—a law of right conduct. Certain actions are under the control of the human will, which is able to rebel against the moral law of nature, and the pagan poet Æschylus traces all human sorrow to "the perverse human will omnipresent."

As birth control means the deliberate frustration of a natural act which might have issued in a new life, it is an unnatural crime, and is stigmatised by theologians as a sin akin to murder. To this charge birth controllers further reply that millions of the elements of procreation are destroyed by Nature herself, and that "to add one more to these millions sacrificed by Nature is surely no crime." This attempt at argument is pathetic. If these people knew even the A.B.C. of biology, they would know that millions of those elements are allowed to perish by Nature for a definite purpose—namely, *to make procreation more certain*. It is in order that the one may achieve the desired end that it is reinforced by millions of others. Moreover, although millions of deaths in the world occur every year from natural causes, it would nevertheless, I fear, be a crime if I were to cause one more death by murdering a birth controller.

§2. REFLECTED IN THE NORMAL CONSCIENCE

In common with irrational animals we have instincts, appetites, and passions; but, unlike the animals, we have the power to reflect whether an action is right or wrong in itself apart from its consequences. This power of moral judgment is called conscience; and it is conscience which reflects the natural law (the Divine Nature expressed in creation). As conscience, when violated, can and does give rise to an unpleasant feeling of shame in the mind, we have good reason to believe that it exists for the purpose of preventing us from doing shameful actions, just as our eyes are intended, amongst other things, to prevent us from walking over precipices. Moreover, if the conscience is active, instructed, and unbiased, it will invariably give the correct answer to any question of right or wrong.

It is possible to assert, without fear of contradiction, that no ordinary decent man or woman approaches or begins the practice of artificial birth control without experiencing at first unpleasant feelings of uneasiness, hesitation, repugnance, shame, and remorse. Later on these feelings may be overcome by habit, for the voice of conscience will cease when it has been frequently ignored. This does not alter the fact that at first the natural moral instincts of both men and women do revolt against these practices. To the conscience of mankind birth control is a shameful action.

§3. EXPRESSED IN THE SCIENCE OF ETHICS

The dictates of conscience go to form the science of ethics. According to ethics, the practice of birth control means the doing of an act whilst at the same time frustrating the object for which the act is intended. It is like using language to conceal the truth, or using appetite so as to injure rather than to promote health. During the decline of the Roman Empire men gorged themselves with food, took an emetic, vomited, and then sat down to eat again. They satiated their appetite and frustrated the object for which appetite is intended. The practice of birth control is parallel to this piggishness. No one can deny that the sexual impulse has for aim the procreation of children. The birth controllers seek to gratify the impulse, yet to defeat the aim; and they are so honest in their mistaken convictions that, when faced with this argument, they boldly adopt an attitude which spells intellectual and moral anarchy. They say that it is simply a waste of time to discuss the moral aspect of this practice. Without being able to dispute the truth that birth control is against nature, conscience, and ethics, they attempt to prove that at any rate the results of this practice are beneficial, or in other words that a good end justifies the use of evil means. This is a doctrine that has been universally repudiated by mankind.[2] Nevertheless, if birth control, in spite of its being an offence against moral and natural law, was really beneficial to humanity, then birth controllers would be able to claim pragmatic justification for the practices, and to argue that what actually and universally tends to the good of mankind cannot be bad in itself. Birth control, as I have already shown, does *not* conform to these conditions; therefore that argument also fails.

§4. BIRTH CONTROL CONDEMNED BY PROTESTANT CHURCHES

The Protestants, at the time of the Reformation, retained and even exaggerated certain beliefs of the undivided Catholic Church. None of them doubted, for instance, that the Bible was the Word of God and therefore a guide to moral conduct. They knew that artificial birth control is forbidden by the Bible, and that in the Old Testament the punishment for that sin was death.[3] In 1876, when Charles Bradlaugh advocated in a notorious pamphlet the practice of birth control, his views were denounced from every Protestant pulpit in the land and were widely repudiated by the upper and middle classes of England. But it would seem that Protestant morality is now disappearing with the spread of indifferentism, and the Protestant Churches have no longer the same influence on the public and private life of the nation. Protestantism has lasted for 400 years, but though it has lasted longer than any other form of belief which took rise in the sixteenth century, it is now also dying.

In 1919 the number of people over seven years of age in England who professed belief in any church was 10,833,795 (out

---

[2] There is, or perhaps we should say there was, a legacy of 1,000 Rhenish guilders awaiting anyone who, in the judgment of the faculty of law in the University of Heidelberg or of Bonn, is able to establish the fact that any Jesuit ever taught this doctrine or anything equivalent to it. Vide *The Antidote*, vol.iii, p. 125, C.T.S., London.

[3] Gen. xxxviii. 9-10.

of 40,000,000), and the church attendance equalled 7,000,000, or about 1 out of every 5 people.[4]

Again, a Commission appointed by the Protestant Churches to inquire into the religious beliefs held in the British armies of the Great War has endorsed the following statements:

> Everyone must be struck with the appalling ignorance of the simplest religious truths. Probably 80 percent of these men from the Midlands had never heard of the sacraments ... It is not only that the men do not know the meaning of 'Church of England'; they are ignorant of the historical facts of the life of our Lord. Nor must it be assumed that this ignorance is confined to men who have passed through the elementary schools. The same verdict is recorded upon those who have been educated in our public schools. ... The men are hopelessly perplexed by the lack of Christian unity.[5]

In my opinion these statements are exaggerations, but that was not the view of the Commission. As regards Scotland, it has recently been stated at the Lothian Synod of the United Free Church that in 1911 at least 37 percent of the men and women of Scotland were without church connection.[6]

In 1870, of every 1,000 marriages, 760 were according to the rites of the Established Church, but in 1919 the proportion had fallen to 597. During the same period civil marriages without religious ceremonial increased from 98 to 231 per 1,000.[7] These figures are an index of the religious complexion of the country. The Protestant Churches are being strangled by the development of a germ that was inherent in them from the beginning, and that growth is Rationalism. The majority of the upper, professional, and artisan class can no longer be claimed as staunch Protestants, but as vague theists; and amongst these educated people, misled by false ideas of pleasure and by pernicious nonsense written about self-realisation, the practice

---

[4] Vide *Catholic Times*, August 27, 1921, p. 7.

[5] *The Army and Religion*, 1919, p. 448.

[6] *Universe*, November 4, 1921, p. 3.

[7] *Eighty-second Annual Report of the Registrar-General of England and Wales*, 1919, p. xxv.

of birth control has spread most alarmingly. This is an evil against which all religious bodies who retain a belief in the fundamental facts of Christianity might surely unite in action.

In a Catholic country there would be no need, in the furtherance of public welfare, to write on the evils of birth control. The teaching of the Catholic Church would be generally accepted, and a moral law generally accepted by the inhabitants of a country gives strength to the State. But Great Britain, no longer Catholic, is now in some danger of ceasing to be even a Christian country. In 1885 it was asserted, "England alone is reported to contain some seven hundred sects, each of whom proves a whole system of theology and morals from the Bible."[8] Each of these that now survives gives its own particular explanation of the law of God, which it honestly tries to follow, but at one point or another each and every sect differs from its neighbours. On account of these differences of opinion many people say: "The Churches cannot agree amongst themselves as to what is truth; they cannot all be right; it is, therefore, impossible for me to know with certainty what to believe; and, to be quite honest, it may save me a lot of bother just at present to have no very firm belief at all." This means that in Great Britain *there is no uniform moral law covering all human conduct and generally accepted by the mass of the people.* As the practice of artificial birth-rate control is not only contrary to Christian morality but is also a menace to the prosperity and well-being of the nation, the absence of a uniform moral law, common to all the people and forbidding this practice, is a source of grave weakness in the State.

---

[8] *The Times*, January 13, 1885.

APPENDIX TO CHAPTER 8
A NEO-MALTHUSIAN ATTACK ON THE CHURCH OF ENGLAND

AS WAS PROVED in a previous chapter artificial birth control was originally based on Atheism, and on a philosophy of moral anarchy. Further proof of this fact is to be found in the course of a most edifying dispute between two rival Neo-Malthusians. This quarrel is between Dr. Marie C. Stopes, President of the Society for Constructive Birth Control and Racial Progress, who is not a Doctor of Medicine but of Philosophy, and Dr. Binnie Dunlop, who is a Bachelor of Medicine: and when birth controllers fall out we may humbly hope that truth will prevail. Dr. Stopes maintains that artificial birth control was not an atheistic movement, whereas Dr. Binnie Dunlop contends that the pioneers of the movement were Atheists. The beginning of the trouble was a letter written by Dr. Stopes to the *British Medical Journal*, in which she made the following statement:

> Dr. Martindale is reported in your pages to have given an address to medical women in which she pointed out that the birth control movement in England dated from the Bradlaugh trial in 1877. Had she attended the presidential address of the Society for Constructive Birth Control she would have learned that there was a very flourishing movement, centring round Dr. Trall in 1866, years before Bradlaugh touched the subject, and also a considerable movement earlier than that. This point is important, as 'birth control' has hitherto (erroneously) been much prejudiced in popular opinion by being supposed to be an atheistical movement originated by Bradlaugh.[1]

Dr. Stopes, who has been working overtime in the attempt to obtain some religious sanction for her propaganda, is ready

---

[1] *British Medical Journal*, November 19, 1921, p. 872.

not only to throw the Atheists overboard, but also to assert that a flourishing movement for artificial birth control centred round the late Dr. Trall, who was a Christian. Her letter was answered by Dr. Binnie Dunlop as follows:

> Dr. Marie C. Stopes, whose valuable books I constantly recommend, protests (page 872) against the statement that the birth control movement in England dated from the trial of Charles Bradlaugh in 1877—for republishing Dr. Knowlton's pamphlet, *The Fruits of Philosophy*, because the Government had interdicted it. She must admit, however, that there was no *organised* movement anywhere until Bradlaugh and the Doctors Drysdale, immediately after the trial, founded the Malthusian League, and that the decline of Europe's birth-rate began in that year. It may now seem unfortunate that the pioneers of the contraceptives idea, from 1818 onwards (James Mill, Francis Place, Richard Carlile, Robert Dale Owen, John Stuart Mill, Dr. Knowlton, Dr. George Drysdale, Dr. C. R. Drysdale, and Charles Bradlaugh), were all Free-thinkers; and Dr. Stopes harps on the religious and praiseworthy Dr. Trall, an American, who published *Sexual Physiology* in 1866. But Dr. Trall was not at all a strong advocate of contraceptive methods. After a brief but helpful reference to the idea of placing a mechanical obstruction, such as a sponge, against the *os uteri*, he said:
>
> 'Let it be distinctly understood that I do not approve any method for preventing pregnancy except that of abstinence, nor any means for producing abortion, on the ground that it is or can be in any sense physiological. It is only the least of two evils. When people will live physiologically there will be no need of preventive measures, nor will there be any need for works of this kind.'[2]

That is a most informative letter. In simple language Dr. Binnie Dunlop tells the remarkable story of how in 1876 three Atheists, merely by forming a little Society in London, were able to cause an immediate fall in the birth-rate of Europe. When you come to think of it, that was a stupendous thing for any three men to have achieved. I am very glad that Dr. Binnie Dunlop has defended the Atheists and has painted the late Dr. Trall, despite

---

[2] *British Medical Journal*, November 26, 1921, p. 924.

that "brief but helpful reference," in his true colours as a Christian. Nevertheless, Dr. Stopes had the last word:

> As regards Dr. Dunlop, he now shifts the Atheists' position by adding the word 'organised.' The Atheists never tire of repeating certain definite misstatements, examples of which are: 'If it were not for the fact that the despised Atheists, Charles Bradlaugh and Annie Besant, faced imprisonment, misrepresentation, insult, and ostracism for this cause forty-four years ago, she [Dr. Stopes] would not be able to conduct her campaign today' (*Literary Guide*, November 1921); and 'Before the Knowlton trial, neither rich nor poor knew anything worth counting about contraceptive devices' (*Malthusian*, November 15, 1921). Variations of these statements have been incessantly made, and I dealt with their contentions in the presidential address for the C.B.C. Meanwhile to them I reply that: 'There has never been in this country any law against the dissemination of properly presented birth control information, and *before, during, and after* the Bradlaugh trial properly presented information on birth control was extending its range with full liberty.' My address is now in the press, and when published will make public not only new matter from manuscript letters of very early date in my possession, but other overlooked historical facts. I have already told Dr. Dunlop I refuse to be drawn into a discussion on facts an account of which is still in the press.[3]

The lady, by her dissertation on the Laws of England, makes a clumsy effort to evade the point at issue, which is quite simple, namely, whether it was Atheists or Christians who initiated the Neo-Malthusian movement, organised or unorganised. Dr. Binnie Dunlop has here proved his case. I also do maintain that in this matter all credit must be given to the Atheists; and that it would be truly contemptible to deny this fact merely in order to pander to a popular prejudice against Atheism. Nor am I shaken in this opinion when Dr. Stopes points out that there was a Neo-Malthusian movement prior to 1876. Of course there was a movement, but it was always an atheistic movement. In the past no Christian doctor, and indeed no Christian man or woman, advocated artificial birth control. Let us give the Neo-Malthusian his due.

---

[3] *British Medical Journal*, December 10, 1921, p. 1,016.

Until recently both the Church of England and the medical profession presented practically a united front against Neo-Malthusian teaching; and, as late as 1914, the Malthusian League did not hesitate to make use of the following calumnies, very mean, very spiteful, very imbecile:

> Take the clergy. They are the officers of a Church that has made marriage a source of revenue and of social control; they preach from a sacred book that bids the chosen people of God 'multiply and replenish the earth'; they know that large families generally tend to preserve clerical influence and authority; and they claim that every baby is a new soul presented to God and, therefore, for His honour and glory, the greatest possible number of souls should be produced.[4]

That feeble attempt to poison the atmosphere was naturally ignored by intelligent people, and more than once Lambeth has ruled that artificial birth control is sin. Unfortunately, within the Church of England, in spite of the Lambeth ruling, there is still discussion as to whether artificial birth control is or is not sin, the Bishops, as a whole, making a loyal effort to uphold Christian teaching against a campaign waged by Malthusians in order to obtain religious sanction for their evil propaganda. Although many Malthusians are rationalists, they are well aware that without some religious sanction their policy could never emerge from the dim underworld of unmentioned and unrespected things and could never be advocated openly in the light of day. To this end birth control is camouflaged by pseudo-poetic and pseudo-religious phraseology, and the Anglican Church is asked to alter her teaching. Birth controllers realise that it is useless to ask this of the Catholic Church, a Rock in their path, but "as regards the Church of England, which makes no claim to infallibility, the case is different, and discussion is possible."[5]

Let us consider, firstly, the teaching of the Church of England on this matter. At the Lambeth Conference of 1908 the Bishops affirmed "that deliberate tampering with nascent life is

---

[4] *Common Sense on the Population Question*, p. 4.
[5] Dr. C. K. Millard, in *The Modern Churchman*, May 1919.

repugnant to Christian morality." In 1914 a Committee of Bishops issued a Memorandum[6] in which artificial birth control is condemned as "dangerous, demoralising, and sinful." The memorandum was approved by a large majority of the Diocesan Bishops, although in the opinion of Dean Inge "this is emphatically a matter in which every man and woman must judge for themselves and must refrain from judging others."[7] The Bishops also held that in some marriages it may be desirable, on grounds of prudence or of health, to limit the number of children. In these circumstances they advised the practice of self-restraint; and, as regards a limited use of marriage, they added the following statement:

> It seems to most of us only a legitimate application of such self-restraint that in certain cases (which only the parties' own judgment and conscience can settle) intercourse should be restricted by consent to certain times at which it is less likely to lead to conception. This is only to use natural conditions, it is approved by good medical authority; it means self-denial and not self-indulgence. And we believe it to be quite legitimate, or at least not to be condemned.

A *small* minority of Bishops held that prolonged or even perpetual abstinence from intercourse is the only legitimate method of limiting a family. Finally, in Resolution 68 of the Lambeth Conference in 1920, the Bishops stated that:

> We utter an emphatic warning against the use of unnatural means for the avoidance of conception, together with the grave dangers—physical, moral, and religious—thereby incurred, and against the evils with which the extension of such use threatens the race. In opposition to the teaching which, under the name of science and religion, encourages married people in the deliberate cultivation of sexual union as an end in itself, we steadfastly uphold what must always be regarded as the governing consideration of Christian marriage. One is the primary purpose for which marriage exists—namely, the continuation of the race through the

---

[6] Reproduced in *The Declining Birth-rate*, 1916, p. 386.
[7] *Outspoken Essays*, 1919, p. 75.

gift and heritage of children; the other is the paramount importance in married life of deliberate and thoughtful self-control.[8]

And the Committee on "Problems of Marriage and Sexual Morality" felt called upon "to utter an earnest warning against the use of any unnatural means by which conception is frustrated."[9]

If Resolution 68 be read in conjunction with the Memorandum of 1914, the teaching of the Church of England is plain to any sane man or woman; it is one with the teaching of the Church Catholic. Artificial birth control is condemned as sin, but, under certain circumstances, the limitation of a family by continence or by *restricted intercourse* is permitted. As this teaching forbids Neo-Malthusian practices, birth controllers have tried to make the Church alter her teaching to suit their opinions. Although their methods in controversy against the Church must be condemned by everyone who values intellectual honesty, the reader, of his charity, should remember that Malthusians are unable to defend their policy, either on logical or on moral grounds. Without attempting to prove that the teaching of the Church is wrong, birth controllers began the attack by *a complete misrepresentation* of what that teaching actually is. This unenviable task was undertaken by Lord Dawson of Penn, at the Birmingham Church Congress of 1921.

After quoting Resolution 68, Lord Dawson said:

> Now the plain meaning of this statement is that sexual union should take place for the sole purpose of procreation, that sexual union as *an* end in itself—not, mind you, *the* only end—(there we should all agree), but sexual union as *an* end in itself is to be condemned.
>
> That means that sexual intercourse should rightly take place *only* for the purpose of procreation.
>
> Quite a large family could easily result from quite a few sexual unions. For the rest the couple should be celibate. Any intercourse not having procreation as its intention is 'sexual union

---

[8] *Report*, p. 44
[9] Ibid., p. 112.

as an end in itself,' and therefore by inference condemned by the Lambeth Conference.

Think of the facts of life. Let us recall our own love—our marriage, our honeymoon. Has not sexual union over and over again been the physical expression of our love without thought or intention of procreation? Have we all been wrong? Or is it that the Church lacks that vital contact with the realities of life which accounts for the gulf between her and the people?

The love envisaged by the Lambeth Conference is an invertebrate, joyless thing—not worth the having. Fortunately it is in contrast to the real thing as practised by clergy and laity.

Fancy an ardent lover (and what respect have you for a lover who is not ardent?)—the type you would like your daughter to marry—virile, ambitious, chivalrous—a man who means to work hard and love hard. Fancy putting before these lovers—eager and expectant of the joys before them—the Lambeth picture of marriage. Do you expect to gain their confidence?[10]

That sort of appeal is not very effective, even as rhetoric; but it is very easy to give an exact parallel. Fancy a fond father (and what respect have you for a father who is not fond?) being told by his daughter's suitor that he, his prospective son-in-law, looked forward to the physical joys of marriage, but intended to insist on his wife using contraceptives. Would any father regard such a one as the type he would like his daughter to marry?

There is, unfortunately, another answer to Lord Dawson, and I put it in the form of a question. Can any intelligent man or woman, Catholic, Protestant, or rationalist, maintain that Lord Dawson has given a fair, a true, or an honest statement of the teaching of the Church of England? Moreover, it is past all understanding how a gross libel on Anglican doctrine has been overlooked by those most concerned. The address is actually hailed as "wise, bold, and humane in the highest sense of the word" by *The Spectator*,[11] and that amazing journal, "expert as ever in making the worse appear the better cause in a way that appeals to clergymen," goes on to say: "Lord Dawson fearlessly and plainly opposed the teachings of the Roman Church and the alleged teachings of the Anglican."

---

[10] *Evening Standard*, October 12, 1921.
[11] October 15, 1921.

Having by a travesty of truth created a false theological bogey, bearing little resemblance either to Catholic or to Anglican teaching, Lord Dawson proceeds to demolish his own creation by a somewhat boisterous eulogy of sex-love. Now sex-love is an instinct and involves no question of good or evil apart from the circumstances in which it is either gratified or denied; but, in view of the freedom with which Lord Dawson discussed this topic, it is only right to note that it was left to the Rev. R. J. Campbell to add to the gaiety of nations by his subsequent protest that the *Marriage Service* "contains expressions which are offensive to modern delicacy of feeling."

That protest is also a first-rate example of the anarchical state of the modern mind. The Rev. R. J. Campbell is a modern mind, so is Mr. George Bernard Shaw; but the latter refers to "the sober decency, earnestness, and authority"[12] of those very passages to which the former objects.

Lord Dawson's eulogy of sexual intercourse was but a prelude to his plea for the use of contraceptives:

> I will next consider Artificial Control. The forces in modern life which make for birth control are so strong that only convincing reasons will make people desist from it. It is said to be unnatural and intrinsically immoral. This word 'unnatural' perplexes me. Why? Civilisation involves the chaining of natural forces and their conversion to man's will and uses. Much of medicine and surgery consists of means to overcome nature.

That paragraph illustrates precisely the confused use of the word "natural," which I have already criticised (Chapter 8). Lord Dawson says he is perplexed, and I agree with him. Civilisation, he says, involves the conversion of natural forces to man's will. So does every crime. Is that any defence of crime? Even if physical nature be described as non-moral, that description cannot be applied to the inward nature of will and conscience. That I will an act may show it is in accordance with nature in a certain sense, but the fact of its being in accordance with physical nature does not justify my act. Does Lord Dawson agree? Or does he think that any action in accordance with the

---

[12] *Man and Superman*, Act III, p. 125.

physical laws of nature, which means any action whatsoever, is justified; and does he approve therefore of mere moral anarchy? His confusion of thought concerning the use of the word "natural" is followed by the inevitable sequence of false analogies:

> When anæsthetics were first used at child-birth there was an outcry on the part of many worthy and religious people that their use under such circumstances was unnatural and wicked, because God meant woman to suffer the struggles and pains of child-birth. Now we all admit it is right to control the process of child-birth, and to save the mother as much pain as possible. It is no more unnatural to control conception by artificial means than to control child-birth by artificial means. Surely the whole question turns on whether these artificial means are for the good or harm of the individual and the community.
>
> Generally speaking, birth control before the first child is inadvisable. On the other hand, the justifiable use of birth control would seem to be to limit the number of children when such is desirable, and to spread out their arrival in such a way as to serve their true interests and those of their home.
>
> Once more, careful distinction needs to be made between the use and the bad effects of the abuse of birth control. That its abuse produces grave harm I fully agree—harm to parents, to families, and to the nation. But abuse is not a just condemnation of legitimate use. Over-eating, over-drinking, over-smoking, over-sleeping, over-work do not carry condemnation of eating, drinking, smoking, sleeping, work.

These long extracts are here quoted because, as *The Spectator* has remarked, "an attempt at a detailed summary might destroy the careful balance which is essential to Lord Dawson's purpose." It might indeed; and many a true word is written inadvertently and despite the wisdom of the serpent. As Lord Dawson believes that Malthusian practice is not of necessity sinful, and as he is urging the Church to remove a ban on that practice, it is necessary for him to prove in the first place that his opinion is right and that the teaching of the Church is wrong. Elsewhere in these pages I have stated *the reasons why* Christian morality brands the *act* of artificial birth control as intrinsically a sin, a *malum in se*, and those reasons have never been disproved by Lord Dawson or by anyone. His comparison between the use of contraceptives and eating or drinking is a false analogy. Eating is a natural act, not in itself sinful, whereas the use of contraceptives is an unnatural act, in itself a sin. The extent to which artificial birth control is practised neither increases nor diminishes the sinful nature of the act, but merely indicates the number of times the same sin is committed. Lord Dawson admits the danger of Neo-Malthusian methods being carried to excess, and counsels that these practices be used in moderation; but is it likely that those who have discarded the teaching of a Church and the dictates of the moral law will be seriously influenced by what he calls "an appeal to patriotism"?

Now there is one appeal to patriotism which Lord Dawson could have made but did not make. He might have pleaded that for the sake of the nation all attempts at unnatural birth control amongst the wealthier and more leisured citizens should be abandoned forthwith, and that the lawful form should be confined to those few cases where limitation of the family is justified on genuine medical grounds. But he refrained from making that appeal, and his plea for the use of contraceptives in moderation is more likely to be quoted with approval in the boudoirs of Mayfair than in humbler homes.

Lord Dawson's grave error in failing to anticipate the inevitable consequences of his deplorable speech is becoming more and more apparent. In the columns of *The Daily Herald*, cheek by jowl with advertisements concerning "Herbalists," "Safe and Sure Treatment for Anæmia, Irregularities, etc.," "Knowledge for Young Wives," and "Surgical Goods and Appliances," there appears the following notice:

> Lord Dawson, the King's Physician, says, 'Birth control has come to stay.' Following up this honest and daring declaration, the Liberator League have decided to distribute 10,000 copies of its publications free to applicants sending stamped addressed envelopes to J. W. Gott, Secretary ... London, N.W.5.

A stamped addressed envelope brought in return sample copies of two undated newsprints, entitled *The Rib Tickler* and *The Liberator*, and, to the honour of newsvendors, we learn that these papers are "not supplied by newsagents." The first print is devoted to Blasphemy, and the second to Birth Control. Both papers are edited by J. W. Gott, "of London, Leeds, Liverpool, and other prisons," who, when he is not in jail for selling blasphemous or obscene literature, earns a livelihood by a propaganda of "Secularism, Socialism, and Neo-Malthusianism," combined with the sale of contraceptives. At Birmingham in 1921 this individual, according to his own statement, was charged, on eleven summonses, with having sent "an obscene book" and "obscene literature" through the post, and with "publishing a blasphemous libel of and concerning the Holy Scriptures and the Christian Religion." "The Malthusian League (at their own expense, for which I here wish to thank them) sent their Hon. Secretary, Dr. Binnie Dunlop, who gave evidence"... that the Council of the Malthusian League .... "most strongly protests against the description of G. Hardy's book, *How to prevent Pregnancy*, as obscene, for that book gives in a perfectly refined and scientific way this urgently needed information." This opinion was not shared by the jury, who brought in a verdict of guilty, and Gott was sentenced to six months' imprisonment. From the *Liberator* we learn that the Treasurer of the Liberator League was fined £20, having been found guilty on the following summons—

> for that you on the eleventh day of September 1920, at the Parish of Consett, in the County aforesaid, unlawfully, wickedly, maliciously, and scandalously did sell to diverse persons, whose names are unknown, in a public street, there situate, a certain lewd, wicked, scandalous, and obscene print entitled 'Large or Small Families,' against the Peace of our Sovereign Lord the King, His Crown and Dignity.

Lord Dawson's advice was indeed perilous because "the British Empire and all its traditions will decline and fall if the Motherland is faithless to motherhood"[13]; and the nation would do better to pay heed to the following words of His Majesty the King: "The foundations of national glory are in the homes of the

---

[13] *Sunday Express*, October 16, 1921.

people. They will only remain unshaken while the family life of our race and nation is strong, simple, and pure."

All Lord Dawson's arguments are hoary fallacies. "Once more, careful distinction needs to be made between"—anæsthetics and contraceptives. Anæsthetics assist the birth of a child, whereas contraceptives frustrate the act of procreation. The old explanation that man's progress has been achieved by harnessing and not by opposing the forces of nature is dismissed with ignominy. The age-long teaching of Hippocrates that the healing art was based on the *Vis Medicatrix Naturae* is overthrown by Lord Dawson of Penn, in a single sentence; and in place of the Father of Medicine as a guide to health of body and mind, there comes the King's Physician "to pestle a poison'd poison behind his crimson lights."

When a great leader announces the birth of a new epoch, it is meet that the rank and file remain silent; and at this Congress of the Church of England no jarring interruptions marred the solemnity of the moment. No old-fashioned doctor was there to utter a futile protest, and there was no simple-minded clergyman to rise in the name of Christ and give Lord Dawson the lie. Without dissent, on a public platform of the Established Church, presided over by a Bishop, and in full view of the nation, "the moth-eaten mantle of Malthus, the godless robe of Bradlaugh, and the discarded garments of Mrs. Besant,"[14] were donned—by the successor of Lister. It was a proud moment for the birth controllers, but for that national institution called "Ecclesia Anglicana" a moment full of shame.

---

[14] On becoming a Theosophist, Mrs. Besant retracted her approval of Neo-Malthusianism.

CHAPTER 9
THE TEACHING OF THE CATHOLIC CHURCH ON BIRTH CONTROL

§1. A FALSE VIEW OF HER DOCTRINE

ONE OF THE MARKS of the Catholic Church, whereby she may be distinguished from all other Churches, is that her teaching is always clear and above all logical. Yet this fact has not saved her teaching from misrepresentation in the hands of Malthusians. For example, Dr. C. Killick Millard writes as follows:

> The Churches have taught that it was the divine wish that human beings should multiply and population increase—the more rapidly the better; the traditional authority for this being the instruction given to Noah and his family, after the Deluge, to 'be fruitful and multiply and replenish the earth.' The Churches have continued to teach that the duty of man was *to obey the divine command* and still *to increase and multiply*, and until recently any attempt by married couples to restrict or regulate the birth-rate was denounced as sinful.
>
> This is still the orthodox attitude, I believe, of the Roman Catholic Church, with its celibate priesthood; but, as it is clearly useless to reason with those who claim infallibility, it is unnecessary to discuss the question further so far as Roman Catholicism is concerned.[1]

Now, although it may be unnecessary for Dr. Millard to discuss the question further, he will, I am sure, regret having inadvertently misstated the truth. The Catholic Church has never denounced as sinful "*any* attempt by married couples to restrict or regulate the birth-rate." On the contrary, the Catholic Church has taught, by her greatest doctor, St. Thomas Aquinas, "that the

---
[1] *The Modern Churchman*, May 1919.

essence of marriage is not primarily in the begetting of offspring, but in the indissoluble union between husband and wife."[2]

§2. THE ESSENCE AND PURPOSE OF MARRIAGE

There is an obvious distinction between the *essence* of a thing and the *ends* or purposes for which the thing exists. For example, in a business partnership the *essence* of the partnership is a legal instrument, whereas the *purposes* or *ends* of the partnership are various commercial projects. The following is a clear statement, by Father Vincent McNabb, O.P.,[3] of Catholic teaching concerning the nature and end of marriage:

> Marriage is an indissoluble state of life wherein a man and a woman agree to give each other power over their bodies for the begetting, birth, and upbringing of offspring. The natural and primary end of marriage is this duty towards offspring. But, as sin has despoiled the human will and disturbed human relations, marriage has now the secondary end of allaying sexual lust.
> But it is a principle of ethics that what is primary cannot be set aside as if it were secondary, nor can the secondary be sought as if it were primary. To invert the ethical order is to bring in that disorder which is called sin. If the human act brings in a slight disorder, it is venial sin; if the human act brings in a grievous disorder it is a grievous or mortal sin.
> It is a grievous disorder, and, therefore, a grievous sin, to desire satisfaction in such sexual intercourse as could not result in the begetting of offspring.
> As the wedded pair have given each other power over their bodies it would be a grave sin for one to refuse either altogether or for a considerable time the fulfilment of the marriage debt. But it is not a sin if by mutual agreement the wedded pair refrain from the marriage debt for a time, or for ever. As a rule, and speaking objectively, it would be heroic virtue for a wedded pair to abstain for a long time, and still more for ever, from the marriage debt. To

---

[2] Rev. Vincent McNabb, O.P., *The Catholic Gazette*, September 1921, p. 194
[3] Ibid.

counsel such a practice indiscriminately would be a sinful want of prudence, and, in a confessor, of professional knowledge.

It is quite clear that by mutual consent, even without any further motive, the wedded pair can abstain from marital intercourse. Still more may they abstain for a time or for ever, for a good motive, e.g. in order to have time for prayer, for good works, for bringing up such family as they already have to support.

§3. ARTIFICIAL STERILITY WHOLLY CONDEMNED

Artificial birth control is an offence against the law of God, and is therefore forbidden by the Catholic Church. Any Catholic who wilfully adopts this practice violates the law of God in a serious matter, and is therefore guilty of mortal sin, an outrageous and deliberate insult offered by a human creature to the Infinite Majesty.

The Catholic Church teaches that men and women should control the sex impulse just as they should control their appetite for food or drink. The principal end of marriage, as we have seen, is the purpose of its institution, the procreation and bringing up of children. The secondary end of marriage is mutual assistance and companionship, and a remedy against concupiscence. Where it is advisable, owing to the health of the mother or owing to reasons of prudence as distinct from selfishness, to limit the number of children, the Catholic Church points out that this should be done by the exercise of self-control, or by restricted use. As those who deny the possibility or even the wisdom of self-restraint are not likely to pay the slightest attention to the teaching of the Church, I will quote the opinions of two clear-thinking, non-Catholic writers.

Mr. George Bernard Shaw has said:

> I have no prejudices. The superstitious view of the Catholic Church is that a priest is something entirely different from an ordinary man. I know a great many Catholic priests, and they are men who have had a great deal of experience. They have at the back a Church which has had for many years to consider the giving of domestic advice to people. If you go to a Catholic priest and tell

him that a life of sexual abstinence means a life of utter misery, he laughs. And obviously for a very good reason. If you go to Westminster Cathedral you will hear voices which sound extremely well, and very differently from the voices of the gentlemen who sing at music-halls, and who would not be able to sing in that way if they did not lead a life extremely different from the Catholic priest....

I may say that I am in favour of birth control. I am in favour of it for its own sake. I do not like to see any human being absolutely the slave of what we used to call 'Nature.' Every human action ought to be controlled, and you make a step in civilisation with something which has been uncontrollable. I am therefore in favour of control for its own sake. But when you go from that to the methods of control, that is a very different thing. As Dr. Routh said, we have to find out methods which will not induce people to declare that they cannot exist without sexual intercourse.[4]

Of course the use of contraceptives is the very negation of self-control.

The late Sir William Osler, speaking of venereal disease, says:

> Personal purity is the prophylaxis which we as physicians are especially bound to advocate. Continence may be a hard condition ... but it can be borne, and it is our duty to urge this lesson upon young and old who seek our advice on matters sexual.

§4. THE ONLY LAWFUL METHOD OF BIRTH CONTROL

There *are* methods of control whereby people are enabled to exist, and to exist happily, without being slaves to the sex impulse. These methods are those of the Catholic Church. Her people are encouraged to take a higher and a nobler view of marriage, to overcome their egoism and selfishness, and to practise moderation and self-restraint in the lawful use of marital rights. The Church urges her people to strengthen their self-restraint by observing the penitential seasons, especially Lent;

---

[4] Speech at the Medico-Legal Society, July 7, 1921.

by fasting or by abstaining from flesh meat at other times, if necessary by abstaining from alcohol; and by seeking that supernatural help which comes to those who receive the Sacraments worthily. When all other deterrents fail, it is lawful, according to the teaching of the Church, for married people to limit intercourse to the mid-menstrual period, when, although conception may occur, it is less likely to occur than at other times.

All other methods are absolutely and without exception forbidden. This limited use of marriage, which, as we have seen, is within the rights of the married, differs from all methods of artificial birth-control as day differs from night, because:

(1) No positive or direct obstacle is used against procreation.

(2) The intercourse is natural, in contradistinction to what is equivalent to self-abuse.

(3) Self-restraint is practised in that the intercourse is limited to certain times.

(4) There is no risk to mental or physical health.

(5) There is no evil will to *defeat* the course of nature; at worst there is merely an absence of heroism.

Even if the question be considered solely as a matter of physiology the difference between these methods is apparent. Physiologists and gynæcologists believe that in natural intercourse there is, apart from fertilisation, an absorption of certain substances into the system of the woman. The role of this absorption is at present obscure, but it obviously exists for a purpose; and it is permissible to speculate whether, under natural conditions of intercourse, there is not a mutual biological reaction that makes, amongst other things, for physical compatibility. Whatever be its purpose or explanation in the marvellous mechanism of nature, this absorption of vital substances is either hindered or is absolutely prevented by artificial methods of birth control; whereas, in the method permitted by the teaching of the Catholic Church there is no interference with a physiological process. Even those who fail, from their lack of training, to comprehend moral distinctions in this matter should be able to appreciate the difference between a method that is physiological and one that is unphysiological.

There are thousands who know little of the Catholic or of any other faith, and thousands who believe the Catholic Church to be everything except what it is. These people have no infallible rule of faith and morals, and when confronted, as they now are, by a dangerous, insidious campaign in favour of birth control, they do not react consistently or at all. It was therefore thought advisable to issue this statement in defence of the position of the Catholic Church; but the reader should remember that the teaching of the Church on this matter is held by her members to be true, not merely because it agrees with the notions of all right-thinking men and women, not because it is in harmony with economic, statistical, social, and biological truth, but principally because they know this teaching to be an authoritative declaration of the law of God. The Ten Commandments have their pragmatic justification; they make for the good of the race; but the Christian obeys them as expressions of the Divine Will.

§5. CONCLUSION

Our declining birth-rate is a fact of the utmost gravity, and a more serious position has never confronted the British people. Here in the midst of a great nation, at the end of a victorious war, the law of decline is working, and by that law the greatest empires in the world have perished. In comparison with that single fact all other dangers, be they of war, of politics, or of disease, are of little moment. Attempts have already been made to avert the consequences by the partial endowment of motherhood and by a saving of infant life. Physiologists are now seeking among the endocrinous glands and the vitamins for a substance to assist procreation. "Where are my children?" was the question shouted yesterday from the cinemas. "Let us have children, children at any price," will be the cry of tomorrow. And all these thoughts were once in the mind of Augustus, Emperor of the world from the Atlantic to the Euphrates, from Mount Atlas to the Danube and the Rhine.

The Catholic Church has never taught that "an avalanche of children" should be brought into the world regardless of consequences. God is not mocked; as men sow, so shall they reap, and against a law of nature both the transient amelioration wrought by philanthropists and the subtle expediences of scientific politicians are alike futile. If our civilisation is to survive we must abandon those ideals that lead to decline. There is only one civilisation immune from decay, and that civilisation endures on the practical eugenics once taught by a united Christendom and now expounded almost solely by the Catholic Church.

BIBLIOGRAPHY

A.—General Publications

Marriage and the Sex Problem. By Dr. F. W. Foerster. Translated by Margaret Booth, B.Sc., Ph.D. London, 1912.
The Menace of the Empty Cradle. By Bernard Vaughan, S.J. London, 1917.
Coffins or Cradles. By Sir James Marchant. 1916.
Moral Principles and Medical Practice. By C. Coppens, S.J., and H. Spalding, S.J.
The Family and the Nation. By W. C. D. Whetham and Mrs. Whetham. London, 1909.
The Law of Births and Deaths. By Charles Edward Pell. London, 1921.
The Declining Birth-rate. Report of the National Birth-rate Commission. London, 1916.
The Church and Labour (A Compendium of Official Utterances). Edited by John A. Ryan, LL.D., and Joseph Husslein, Ph.D. London, 1921.

B.—Catholic Truth Society Publications

The Condition of the Working Classes. (The Encyclical Rerum Novarum.) By Pope Leo XIII. Edited by Mgr. Canon Parkinson, D.D.
Social Questions and the Duty of Catholics. By C. S. Devas, M.A.
Birth-rate, The Declining. By H. Thurston, S.J.
Christian Democracy before the Reformation. By Cardinal Gasquet, O.S.B.
Christian Democracy: Its Meaning and Aim. By C. S. Devas.
Christian Womanhood.

Church and Social Reformers, The. By the Bishop of Northampton.
Conjugal Life, The Duties of. By Cardinal Mercier.
Divorce. By the Bishop of Northampton.
English Economics and Catholic Ethics. By M. Maher.
Labour, The Church and. By Abbot Snow, O.S.B.
Landlords, A Dialogue on. By R. P. Garrold, S.J.
The Catholic Church and the Principle of Private Property. By Hilaire Belloc.
Rome and the Social Question.
Social Reform, Pope Pius X on.
Social Sense, The: Its Decay and its Revival. By A. P. Mooney, M.D.
Socialism, The Catholic Church and. By Hilaire Belloc.
Socialism, An Examination of. By the same.
Socialism, Some Ethical Criticisms of. By A. P. Mooney, M.D.
Trade Unionism. By Henry Somerville.
Woman in the Catholic Church. By H. F. Hall.
The Church and Science. By Sir Bertram Windle, M.D., F.R.S., K.S.G.
Twelve Catholic Men of Science. Edited by Sir Bertram Windle, M.D., F.R.S. Sir Dominic Corrigan—Thomas Dwight—Galvani—Lapparent—Laennec—Linacre—Mendel—Johannes Müller—Pasteur—Secchi—Nicolaus Stenson—Vesalius.
Facts and Theories. A Consideration of Some Biological Conceptions of Today. By Sir Bertram Windle, M.D., F.R.S., K.S.G.
The Modernist. By Joseph Rickaby, S.J.
The World and Its Maker. By J. Gerard, S.J.
Anti-Catholic History: How it is written. By Hilaire Belloc.
Darwinism, The Decline of. By Walter Sweetman.
Evolution and Exact Thought. By J. Gerard, S.J.
Freedom of Thought. By J. Vance, M.A., Ph.D.
Freethought, Modern. By J. Gerard, S.J., F.L.S.
Haeckel and his Philosophy. By J. Gerard, S.J.
Life, The Origin of. By J. Gerard, S.J., F.L.S.
Positivism. By Joseph Rickaby, S.J.

Rationalist Propaganda, The, and How it must be met. By J. Gerard, S.J.
Rationalist, The (Joseph McCabe), as Prophet. By J. Keating, S.J.
Science and Its Counterfeit. By J. Gerard, S.J.
Science or Romance: The Game of Speculation. By J. Gerard, S.J.
Scientific Facts and Scientific Hypotheses. By Sir Bertram Windle, M.D., F.R.S.
Scientific Opinion, The Ebb and Flow of. By Sir Bertram Windle, M.D., F.R.S.
Babylonia and Assyria. By A. Condamin, S.J.
The Catholic Church. By Canon Gildea.
France, Plain Words on Church and State in.
France, The Real Authors of the Separation in. By O. Kellet, S.J.
"Good Queen Bess," The Days of. By William Cobbett.
Kulturkampf, The. By Humphrey Johnson, B.A.
Luther, Four Centuries of. By Canon William Barry, D.D.
Mediæval England, Catholic Faith and Practice in. By H. J. Kilduff.
Monasteries, The Suppression of the English. By William Cobbett.
The Pilgrim Fathers. By H. Thurston, S.J.
Reformation, Social Effects of the. By William Cobbett.
Do Babies build Slums? By Halliday Sutherland, M.D.

C.—Catholic Social Guild Publications

A Primer of Social Science. By Mgr. Parkinson.
Prostitution: The Moral Bearings of the Problem. By M. F. and J. F. Foreword by the late Archbishop of Liverpool.
The Church and Eugenics. (New and revised edition, 1921.) By T. Gerrard.
The Christian Family. By Margaret Fletcher.
Sweated Labour and the Trade Boards Act. Edited by T. Wright.
Guild Socialism. A Criticism of the National Guild Theory. By Francis Goldwell.

Elements of Housing. By C. Tigar, S.J.
The Gospel and the Citizen. By C. C. Martindale, S.J.
The Church and the Worker. By V. M. Crawford.
Questions of the Day. By J. Keating, S.J., and S. A. Parker, O.S.B.
Elements of Economics. By Lewish Watt, S.J.
The Nation's Crisis. By Cardinal Bourne.
The Catholic Attitude to the Ministry of Health. By J. B. McLaughlin, O.S.B., and A. P. Mooney, M.D.

D.—French Publications

La Dépopulation de la France. Jacques Bertillon. 1911.
La Population française. Levasseur. 1891.
La Question de la population. Leroy-Beaulieu.
Dépopulation et Civilisation. 1890. Arsène Dumont.
Natalie. Dr. Bertillon Père.

APPENDIX: *HUMANAE VITAE*

ENCYCLICAL LETTER
HUMANAE VITAE
OF THE SUPREME PONTIFF
PAUL VI
TO HIS VENERABLE BROTHERS
THE PATRIARCHS, ARCHBISHOPS, BISHOPS
AND OTHER LOCAL ORDINARIES
IN PEACE AND COMMUNION WITH THE
APOSTOLIC SEE,
TO THE CLERGY AND FAITHFUL OF THE WHOLE
CATHOLIC WORLD, AND TO ALL MEN OF GOOD
WILL,
ON THE REGULATION OF BIRTH

Honored Brothers and Dear Sons,
Health and Apostolic Benediction.

The transmission of human life is a most serious role in which married people collaborate freely and responsibly with God the Creator. It has always been a source of great joy to them, even though it sometimes entails many difficulties and hardships.

The fulfillment of this duty has always posed problems to the conscience of married people, but the recent course of human society and the concomitant changes have provoked new questions. The Church cannot ignore these questions, for they concern matters intimately connected with the life and happiness of human beings.

I.
PROBLEM AND COMPETENCY OF THE MAGISTERIUM

2. The changes that have taken place are of considerable importance and varied in nature. In the first place there is the rapid increase in population which has made many fear that world population is going to grow faster than available resources, with the consequence that many families and developing countries would be faced with greater hardships. This can easily induce public authorities to be tempted to take even harsher measures to avert this danger. There is also the fact that not only working and housing conditions but the greater demands made both in the economic and educational field pose a living situation in which it is frequently difficult these days to provide properly for a large family.

Also noteworthy is a new understanding of the dignity of woman and her place in society, of the value of conjugal love in marriage and the relationship of conjugal acts to this love.

But the most remarkable development of all is to be seen in man's stupendous progress in the domination and rational organization of the forces of nature to the point that he is endeavoring to extend this control over every aspect of his own life—over his body, over his mind and emotions, over his social life, and even over the laws that regulate the transmission of life.

New Questions

3. This new state of things gives rise to new questions. Granted the conditions of life today and taking into account the relevance of married love to the harmony and mutual fidelity of husband and wife, would it not be right to review the moral norms in force till now, especially when it is felt that these can be observed only with the gravest difficulty, sometimes only by heroic effort?

Moreover, if one were to apply here the so called principle of totality, could it not be accepted that the intention to have a less prolific but more rationally planned family might transform an action which renders natural processes infertile into a licit and provident control of birth? Could it not be admitted, in other words, that procreative finality applies to the totality of married life rather than to each single act? A further question is whether, because people are more conscious today of their responsibilities, the time has not come when the transmission of life should be regulated by their intelligence and will rather than through the specific rhythms of their own bodies.

Interpreting the Moral Law

4. This kind of question requires from the teaching authority of the Church a new and deeper reflection on the principles of the moral teaching on marriage—a teaching which is based on the natural law as illuminated and enriched by divine Revelation.

No member of the faithful could possibly deny that the Church is competent in her magisterium to interpret the natural moral law. It is in fact indisputable, as Our predecessors have many times declared, (1) that Jesus Christ, when He communicated His divine power to Peter and the other Apostles and sent them to teach all nations His commandments, (2) constituted them as the authentic guardians and interpreters of the whole moral law, not only, that is, of the law of the Gospel but also of the natural law. For the natural law, too, declares the will of God, and its faithful observance is necessary for men's eternal salvation. (3)

In carrying out this mandate, the Church has always issued appropriate documents on the nature of marriage, the correct use of conjugal rights, and the duties of spouses. These documents have been more copious in recent times. (4)

Special Studies

5. The consciousness of the same responsibility induced Us to confirm and expand the commission set up by Our predecessor Pope John XXIII, of happy memory, in March, 1963. This commission included married couples as well as many experts in the various fields pertinent to these questions. Its task was to examine views and opinions concerning married life, and especially on the correct regulation of births; and it was also to provide the teaching authority of the Church with such evidence as would enable it to give an apt reply in this matter, which not only the faithful but also the rest of the world were waiting for. (5)

When the evidence of the experts had been received, as well as the opinions and advice of a considerable number of Our brethren in the episcopate—some of whom sent their views spontaneously, while others were requested by Us to do so—We were in a position to weigh with more precision all the aspects of this complex subject. Hence We are deeply grateful to all those concerned.

The Magisterium's Reply

6. However, the conclusions arrived at by the commission could not be considered by Us as definitive and absolutely certain, dispensing Us from the duty of examining personally this serious question. This was all the more necessary because, within the commission itself, there was not complete agreement concerning the moral norms to be proposed, and especially because certain approaches and criteria for a solution to this question had emerged which were at variance with the moral doctrine on marriage constantly taught by the magisterium of the Church.

Consequently, now that We have sifted carefully the evidence sent to Us and intently studied the whole matter, as well as prayed constantly to God, We, by virtue of the mandate entrusted to Us by Christ, intend to give Our reply to this series of grave questions.

II.
DOCTRINAL PRINCIPLES

7. The question of human procreation, like every other question which touches human life, involves more than the limited aspects specific to such disciplines as biology, psychology, demography or sociology. It is the whole man and the whole mission to which he is called that must be considered: both its natural, earthly aspects and its supernatural, eternal aspects. And since in the attempt to justify artificial methods of birth control many appeal to the demands of married love or of responsible parenthood, these two important realities of married life must be accurately defined and analyzed. This is what We mean to do, with special reference to what the Second Vatican Council taught with the highest authority in its Pastoral Constitution on the Church in the World of Today.

God's Loving Design

8. Married love particularly reveals its true nature and nobility when we realize that it takes its origin from God, who "is love," (6) the Father "from whom every family in heaven and on earth is named." (7)

Marriage, then, is far from being the effect of chance or the result of the blind evolution of natural forces. It is in reality the wise and provident institution of God the Creator, whose purpose was to effect in man His loving design. As a consequence, husband and wife, through that mutual gift of themselves, which is specific and exclusive to them alone, develop that union of two persons in which they perfect one another, cooperating with God in the generation and rearing of new lives.

The marriage of those who have been baptized is, in addition, invested with the dignity of a sacramental sign of grace, for it represents the union of Christ and His Church.

Married Love

9. In the light of these facts the characteristic features and exigencies of married love are clearly indicated, and it is of the highest importance to evaluate them exactly.

This love is above all fully human, a compound of sense and spirit. It is not, then, merely a question of natural instinct or emotional drive. It is also, and above all, an act of the free will, whose trust is such that it is meant not only to survive the joys and sorrows of daily life, but also to grow, so that husband and wife become in a way one heart and one soul, and together attain their human fulfillment.

It is a love which is total—that very special form of personal friendship in which husband and wife generously share everything, allowing no unreasonable exceptions and not thinking solely of their own convenience. Whoever really loves his partner loves not only for what he receives, but loves that partner for the partner's own sake, content to be able to enrich the other with the gift of himself.

Married love is also faithful and exclusive of all other, and this until death. This is how husband and wife understood it on the day on which, fully aware of what they were doing, they freely vowed themselves to one another in marriage. Though this fidelity of husband and wife sometimes presents difficulties, no one has the right to assert that it is impossible; it is, on the contrary, always honorable and meritorious. The example of countless married couples proves not only that fidelity is in accord with the nature of marriage, but also that it is the source of profound and enduring happiness.

Finally, this love is fecund. It is not confined wholly to the loving interchange of husband and wife; it also contrives to go beyond this to bring new life into being. "Marriage and conjugal love are by their nature ordained toward the procreation and education of children. Children are really the supreme gift of marriage and contribute in the highest degree to their parents' welfare." (8)

Responsible Parenthood

10. Married love, therefore, requires of husband and wife the full awareness of their obligations in the matter of responsible parenthood, which today, rightly enough, is much insisted upon, but which at the same time should be rightly understood. Thus, we do well to consider responsible parenthood in the light of its varied legitimate and interrelated aspects.

With regard to the biological processes, responsible parenthood means an awareness of, and respect for, their proper functions.

In the procreative faculty the human mind discerns biological laws that apply to the human person. (9)

With regard to man's innate drives and emotions, responsible parenthood means that man's reason and will must exert control over them.

With regard to physical, economic, psychological and social conditions, responsible parenthood is exercised by those who prudently and generously decide to have more children, and by those who, for serious reasons and with due respect to moral precepts, decide not to have additional children for either a certain or an indefinite period of time.

Responsible parenthood, as we use the term here, has one further essential aspect of paramount importance. It concerns the objective moral order which was established by God, and of which a right conscience is the true interpreter. In a word, the exercise of responsible parenthood requires that husband and wife, keeping a right order of priorities, recognize their own duties toward God, themselves, their families and human society.

From this it follows that they are not free to act as they choose in the service of transmitting life, as if it were wholly up to them to decide what is the right course to follow. On the contrary, they are bound to ensure that what they do corresponds to the will of God the Creator. The very nature of marriage and its use makes His will clear, while the constant teaching of the Church spells it out. (10)

Observing the Natural Law

11. The sexual activity, in which husband and wife are intimately and chastely united with one another, through which human life is transmitted, is, as the recent Council recalled, "noble and worthy." (11) It does not, moreover, cease to be legitimate even when, for reasons independent of their will, it is foreseen to be infertile. For its natural adaptation to the expression and strengthening of the union of husband and wife is not thereby suppressed. The fact is, as experience shows, that new life is not the result of each and every act of sexual intercourse. God has wisely ordered laws of nature and the incidence of fertility in such a way that successive births are already naturally spaced through the inherent operation of these laws. The Church, nevertheless, in urging men to the observance of the precepts of the natural law, which it interprets by its constant doctrine, teaches that each and every marital act must of necessity retain its intrinsic relationship to the procreation of human life. (12)

Union and Procreation

12. This particular doctrine, often expounded by the magisterium of the Church, is based on the inseparable connection, established by God, which man on his own initiative may not break, between the unitive significance and the procreative significance which are both inherent to the marriage act.

The reason is that the fundamental nature of the marriage act, while uniting husband and wife in the closest intimacy, also renders them capable of generating new life—and this as a result of laws written into the actual nature of man and of woman. And if each of these essential qualities, the unitive and the procreative, is preserved, the use of marriage fully retains its sense of true mutual love and its ordination to the supreme responsibility of parenthood to which man is called. We believe that our contemporaries are particularly capable of seeing that this teaching is in harmony with human reason.

Faithfulness to God's Design

13. Men rightly observe that a conjugal act imposed on one's partner without regard to his or her condition or personal and reasonable wishes in the matter, is no true act of love, and therefore offends the moral order in its particular application to the intimate relationship of husband and wife. If they further reflect, they must also recognize that an act of mutual love which impairs the capacity to transmit life which God the Creator, through specific laws, has built into it, frustrates His design which constitutes the norm of marriage, and contradicts the will of the Author of life. Hence to use this divine gift while depriving it, even if only partially, of its meaning and purpose, is equally repugnant to the nature of man and of woman, and is consequently in opposition to the plan of God and His holy will. But to experience the gift of married love while respecting the laws of conception is to acknowledge that one is not the master of the sources of life but rather the minister of the design established by the Creator. Just as man does not have unlimited dominion over his body in general, so also, and with more particular reason, he has no such dominion over his specifically sexual faculties, for these are concerned by their very nature with the generation of life, of which God is the source. "Human life is sacred—all men must recognize that fact," Our predecessor Pope John XXIII recalled. "From its very inception it reveals the creating hand of God." (13)

Unlawful Birth Control Methods

14. Therefore We base Our words on the first principles of a human and Christian doctrine of marriage when We are obliged once more to declare that the direct interruption of the generative process already begun and, above all, all direct abortion, even for therapeutic reasons, are to be absolutely excluded as lawful means of regulating the number of children. (14) Equally to be condemned, as the magisterium of the Church has affirmed on many occasions, is direct sterilization, whether of the man or of the woman, whether permanent or temporary. (15)

Similarly excluded is any action which either before, at the moment of, or after sexual intercourse, is specifically intended to prevent procreation—whether as an end or as a means. (16)

Neither is it valid to argue, as a justification for sexual intercourse which is deliberately contraceptive, that a lesser evil is to be preferred to a greater one, or that such intercourse would merge with procreative acts of past and future to form a single entity, and so be qualified by exactly the same moral goodness as these. Though it is true that sometimes it is lawful to tolerate a lesser moral evil in order to avoid a greater evil or in order to promote a greater good," it is never lawful, even for the gravest reasons, to do evil that good may come of it (18)—in other words, to intend directly something which of its very nature contradicts the moral order, and which must therefore be judged unworthy of man, even though the intention is to protect or promote the welfare of an individual, of a family or of society in general. Consequently, it is a serious error to think that a whole married life of otherwise normal relations can justify sexual intercourse which is deliberately contraceptive and so intrinsically wrong.

Lawful Therapeutic Means

15. On the other hand, the Church does not consider at all illicit the use of those therapeutic means necessary to cure bodily diseases, even if a foreseeable impediment to procreation should result there from—provided such impediment is not directly intended for any motive whatsoever. (19)

Recourse to Infertile Periods

16. Now as We noted earlier (no. 3), some people today raise the objection against this particular doctrine of the Church concerning the moral laws governing marriage, that human intelligence has both the right and responsibility to control those forces of irrational nature which come within its ambit and to direct them toward ends beneficial to man. Others ask on the same point whether it is not reasonable in so many cases to use artificial birth control if by so doing the harmony and peace of a family are better served and more suitable conditions are provided for the education of children already born. To this question We must give a clear reply. The Church is the first to praise and commend the application of human intelligence to an activity in which a rational creature such as man is so closely associated with his Creator. But she affirms that this must be done within the limits of the order of reality established by God.

If therefore there are well-grounded reasons for spacing births, arising from the physical or psychological condition of husband or wife, or from external circumstances, the Church teaches that married people may then take advantage of the natural cycles immanent in the reproductive system and engage in marital intercourse only during those times that are infertile, thus controlling birth in a way which does not in the least offend the moral principles which We have just explained. (20)

Neither the Church nor her doctrine is inconsistent when she considers it lawful for married people to take advantage of the infertile period but condemns as always unlawful the use of means which directly prevent conception, even when the reasons given for the later practice may appear to be upright and serious. In reality, these two cases are completely different. In the former the married couple rightly use a faculty provided them by nature. In the later they obstruct the natural development of the generative process. It cannot be denied that in each case the married couple, for acceptable reasons, are both perfectly clear in their intention to avoid children and wish to make sure that none will result. But it is equally true that it is exclusively in the former case that husband and wife are ready to abstain from intercourse during the fertile period as often as for reasonable motives the birth of another child is not desirable. And when the infertile period recurs, they use their married intimacy to express their mutual love and safeguard their fidelity toward one another. In doing this they certainly give proof of a true and authentic love.

Consequences of Artificial Methods

17. Responsible men can become more deeply convinced of the truth of the doctrine laid down by the Church on this issue if they reflect on the consequences of methods and plans for artificial birth control. Let them first consider how easily this course of action could open wide the way for marital infidelity and a general lowering of moral standards. Not much experience is needed to be fully aware of human weakness and to understand that human beings—and especially the young, who are so exposed to temptation—need incentives to keep the moral law, and it is an evil thing to make it easy for them to break that law.

Another effect that gives cause for alarm is that a man who grows accustomed to the use of contraceptive methods may forget the reverence due to a woman, and, disregarding her physical and emotional equilibrium, reduce her to being a mere instrument for the satisfaction of his own desires, no longer considering her as his partner whom he should surround with care and affection.

Finally, careful consideration should be given to the danger of this power passing into the hands of those public authorities who care little for the precepts of the moral law. Who will blame a government which in its attempt to resolve the problems affecting an entire country resorts to the same measures as are regarded as lawful by married people in the solution of a particular family difficulty? Who will prevent public authorities from favoring those contraceptive methods which they consider more effective? Should they regard this as necessary, they may even impose their use on everyone. It could well happen, therefore, that when people, either individually or in family or social life, experience the inherent difficulties of the divine law and are determined to avoid them, they may give into the hands of public authorities the power to intervene in the most personal and intimate responsibility of husband and wife.

Limits to Man's Power

Consequently, unless we are willing that the responsibility of procreating life should be left to the arbitrary decision of men, we must accept that there are certain limits, beyond which it is wrong to go, to the power of man over his own body and its natural functions—limits, let it be said, which no one, whether as a private individual or as a public authority, can lawfully exceed. These limits are expressly imposed because of the reverence due to the whole human organism and its natural functions, in the light of the principles We stated earlier, and in accordance with a correct understanding of the "principle of totality" enunciated by Our predecessor Pope Pius XII. (21)

Concern of the Church

18. It is to be anticipated that perhaps not everyone will easily accept this particular teaching. There is too much clamorous outcry against the voice of the Church, and this is intensified by modern means of communication. But it comes as no surprise to the Church that she, no less than her divine Founder, is destined to be a "sign of contradiction." (22) She does not, because of this, evade the duty imposed on her of proclaiming humbly but firmly the entire moral law, both natural and evangelical.

Since the Church did not make either of these laws, she cannot be their arbiter—only their guardian and interpreter. It could never be right for her to declare lawful what is in fact unlawful, since that, by its very nature, is always opposed to the true good of man.

In preserving intact the whole moral law of marriage, the Church is convinced that she is contributing to the creation of a truly human civilization. She urges man not to betray his personal responsibilities by putting all his faith in technical expedients. In this way she defends the dignity of husband and wife. This course of action shows that the Church, loyal to the example and teaching of the divine Savior, is sincere and unselfish in her regard for men whom she strives to help even now during this earthly pilgrimage "to share God's life as sons of the living God, the Father of all men." (23)

III.
PASTORAL DIRECTIVES

19. Our words would not be an adequate expression of the thought and solicitude of the Church, Mother and Teacher of all peoples, if, after having recalled men to the observance and respect of the divine law regarding matrimony, they did not also support mankind in the honest regulation of birth amid the difficult conditions which today afflict families and peoples. The Church, in fact, cannot act differently toward men than did the Redeemer. She knows their weaknesses, she has compassion on the multitude, she welcomes sinners. But at the same time she cannot do otherwise than teach the law. For it is in fact the law of human life restored to its native truth and guided by the Spirit of God. (24) Observing the Divine Law.

20. The teaching of the Church regarding the proper regulation of birth is a promulgation of the law of God Himself. And yet there is no doubt that to many it will appear not merely difficult but even impossible to observe. Now it is true that like all good things which are outstanding for their nobility and for the benefits which they confer on men, so this law demands from individual men and women, from families and from human society, a resolute purpose and great endurance. Indeed it cannot be observed unless God comes to their help with the grace by which the goodwill of men is sustained and strengthened. But to those who consider this matter diligently it will indeed be evident that this endurance enhances man's dignity and confers benefits on human society.

Value of Self-Discipline

21. The right and lawful ordering of birth demands, first of all, that spouses fully recognize and value the true blessings of family life and that they acquire complete mastery over themselves and their emotions. For if with the aid of reason and of free will they are to control their natural drives, there can be no doubt at all of the need for self-denial. Only then will the expression of love, essential to married life, conform to right order. This is especially clear in the practice of periodic continence. Self-discipline of this kind is a shining witness to the chastity of husband and wife and, far from being a hindrance to their love of one another, transforms it by giving it a more truly human character. And if this self-discipline does demand that they persevere in their purpose and efforts, it has at the same time the salutary effect of enabling husband and wife to develop to their personalities and to be enriched with spiritual blessings. For it brings to family life abundant fruits of tranquility and peace. It helps in solving difficulties of other kinds. It fosters in husband and wife thoughtfulness and loving consideration for one another. It helps them to repel inordinate self-love, which is the opposite of charity. It arouses in them a consciousness of their responsibilities. And finally, it confers upon parents a deeper and more effective influence in the education of their children. As their children grow up, they develop a right sense of values and achieve a serene and harmonious use of their mental and physical powers.

Promotion of Chastity

22. We take this opportunity to address those who are engaged in education and all those whose right and duty it is to provide for the common good of human society. We would call their attention to the need to create an atmosphere favorable to the growth of chastity so that true liberty may prevail over license and the norms of the moral law may be fully safeguarded.

Everything therefore in the modern means of social communication which arouses men's baser passions and encourages low moral standards, as well as every obscenity in the written word and every form of indecency on the stage and screen, should be condemned publicly and unanimously by all those who have at heart the advance of civilization and the safeguarding of the outstanding values of the human spirit. It is quite absurd to defend this kind of depravity in the name of art or culture (25) or by pleading the liberty which may be allowed in this field by the public authorities.

Appeal to Public Authorities

23. And now We wish to speak to rulers of nations. To you most of all is committed the responsibility of safeguarding the common good. You can contribute so much to the preservation of morals. We beg of you, never allow the morals of your peoples to be undermined. The family is the primary unit in the state; do not tolerate any legislation which would introduce into the family those practices which are opposed to the natural law of God. For there are other ways by which a government can and should solve the population problem—that is to say by enacting laws which will assist families and by educating the people wisely so that the moral law and the freedom of the citizens are both safeguarded.

Seeking True Solutions

We are fully aware of the difficulties confronting the public authorities in this matter, especially in the developing countries. In fact, We had in mind the justifiable anxieties which weigh upon them when We published Our encyclical letter *Populorum Progressio*. But now We join Our voice to that of Our predecessor John XXIII of venerable memory, and We make Our own his words: "No statement of the problem and no solution to it is acceptable which does violence to man's essential dignity; those who propose such solutions base them on an utterly materialistic conception of man himself and his life. The only possible solution to this question is one which envisages the social and economic progress both of individuals and of the whole of human society, and which respects and promotes true human values." (26) No one can, without being grossly unfair, make divine Providence responsible for what clearly seems to be the result of misguided governmental policies, of an insufficient sense of social justice, of a selfish accumulation of material goods, and finally of a culpable failure to undertake those initiatives and responsibilities which would raise the standard of living of peoples and their children. (27) If only all governments which were able would do what some are already doing so nobly, and bestir themselves to renew their efforts and their undertakings! There must be no relaxation in the programs of mutual aid between all the branches of the great human family. Here We believe an almost limitless field lies open for the activities of the great international institutions.

To Scientists

24. Our next appeal is to men of science. These can "considerably advance the welfare of marriage and the family and also peace of conscience, if by pooling their efforts they strive to elucidate more thoroughly the conditions favorable to a proper regulation of births." (28) It is supremely desirable, and this was also the mind of Pius XII, that medical science should by the study of natural rhythms succeed in determining a sufficiently secure basis for the chaste limitation of offspring. (29) In this way scientists, especially those who are Catholics, will by their research establish the truth of the Church's claim that "there can be no contradiction between two divine laws—that which governs the transmitting of life and that which governs the fostering of married love." (30)

To Christian Couples

25. And now We turn in a special way to Our own sons and daughters, to those most of all whom God calls to serve Him in the state of marriage. While the Church does indeed hand on to her children the inviolable conditions laid down by God's law, she is also the herald of salvation and through the sacraments she flings wide open the channels of grace through which man is made a new creature responding in charity and true freedom to the design of his Creator and Savior, experiencing too the sweetness of the yoke of Christ. (31)

In humble obedience then to her voice, let Christian husbands and wives be mindful of their vocation to the Christian life, a vocation which, deriving from their Baptism, has been confirmed anew and made more explicit by the Sacrament of Matrimony. For by this sacrament they are strengthened and, one might almost say, consecrated to the faithful fulfillment of their duties. Thus will they realize to the full their calling and bear witness as becomes them, to Christ before the world. (32) For the Lord has entrusted to them the task of making visible to men and women the holiness and joy of the law which united inseparably their love for one another and the cooperation they give to God's love, God who is the Author of human life.

We have no wish at all to pass over in silence the difficulties, at times very great, which beset the lives of Christian married couples. For them, as indeed for every one of us, "the gate is narrow and the way is hard, that leads to life." (33) Nevertheless it is precisely the hope of that life which, like a brightly burning torch, lights up their journey, as, strong in spirit, they strive to live "sober, upright and godly lives in this world," (34) knowing for sure that "the form of this world is passing away." (35)

Recourse to God

For this reason husbands and wives should take up the burden appointed to them, willingly, in the strength of faith and of that hope which "does not disappoint us, because God's love has been poured into our hearts through the Holy Spirit who has been given to us ~}36 Then let them implore the help of God with unremitting prayer and, most of all, let them draw grace and charity from that unfailing fount which is the Eucharist. If, however, sin still exercises its hold over them, they are not to lose heart. Rather must they, humble and persevering, have recourse to the mercy of God, abundantly bestowed in the Sacrament of Penance. In this way, for sure, they will be able to reach that perfection of married life which the Apostle sets out in these words: "Husbands, love your wives, as Christ loved the Church. . . Even so husbands should love their wives as their own bodies. He who loves his wife loves himself. For no man ever hates his own flesh, but nourishes and cherishes it, as Christ does the Church. . . This is a great mystery, and I mean in reference to Christ and the Church; however, let each one of you love his wife as himself, and let the wife see that she respects her husband." (37)

Family Apostolate

26. Among the fruits that ripen if the law of God be resolutely obeyed, the most precious is certainly this, that married couples themselves will often desire to communicate their own experience to others. Thus it comes about that in the fullness of the lay vocation will be included a novel and outstanding form of the apostolate by which, like ministering to like, married couples themselves by the leadership they offer will become apostles to other married couples. And surely among all the forms of the Christian apostolate it is hard to think of one more opportune for the present time. (38)

To Doctors and Nurses

27. Likewise we hold in the highest esteem those doctors and members of the nursing profession who, in the exercise of their calling, endeavor to fulfill the demands of their Christian vocation before any merely human interest. Let them therefore continue constant in their resolution always to support those lines of action which accord with faith and with right reason. And let them strive to win agreement and support for these policies among their professional colleagues. Moreover, they should regard it as an essential part of their skill to make themselves fully proficient in this difficult field of medical knowledge. For then, when married couples ask for their advice, they may be in a position to give them right counsel and to point them in the proper direction. Married couples have a right to expect this much from them.

To Priests

28. And now, beloved sons, you who are priests, you who in virtue of your sacred office act as counselors and spiritual leaders both of individual men and women and of families—We turn to you filled with great confidence. For it is your principal duty—We are speaking especially to you who teach moral theology—to spell out clearly and completely the Church's teaching on marriage. In the performance of your ministry you must be the first to give an example of that sincere obedience, inward as well as outward, which is due to the magisterium of the Church. For, as you know, the pastors of the Church enjoy a special light of the Holy Spirit in teaching the truth. (39) And this, rather than the arguments they put forward, is why you are bound to such obedience. Nor will it escape you that if men's peace of soul and the unity of the Christian people are to be preserved, then it is of the utmost importance that in moral as well as in dogmatic theology all should obey the magisterium of the Church and should speak as with one voice. Therefore We make Our own the anxious words of the great Apostle Paul and with all Our heart We renew Our appeal to you: "I appeal to you, brethren, by the name of our Lord Jesus Christ, that all of you agree and that there be no dissensions among you, but that you be united in the same mind and the same judgment." (40)

Christian Compassion

29. Now it is an outstanding manifestation of charity toward souls to omit nothing from the saving doctrine of Christ; but this must always be joined with tolerance and charity, as Christ Himself showed in His conversations and dealings with men. For when He came, not to judge, but to save the world, (41) was He not bitterly severe toward sin, but patient and abounding in mercy toward sinners?

Husbands and wives, therefore, when deeply distressed by reason of the difficulties of their life, must find stamped in the heart and voice of their priest the likeness of the voice and the love of our Redeemer.

So speak with full confidence, beloved sons, convinced that while the Holy Spirit of God is present to the magisterium proclaiming sound doctrine, He also illumines from within the hearts of the faithful and invites their assent. Teach married couples the necessary way of prayer and prepare them to approach more often with great faith the Sacraments of the Eucharist and of Penance. Let them never lose heart because of their weakness.

To Bishops

30. And now as We come to the end of this encyclical letter, We turn Our mind to you, reverently and lovingly, beloved and venerable brothers in the episcopate, with whom We share more closely the care of the spiritual good of the People of God. For We invite all of you, We implore you, to give a lead to your priests who assist you in the sacred ministry, and to the faithful of your dioceses, and to devote yourselves with all zeal and without delay to safeguarding the holiness of marriage, in order to guide married life to its full human and Christian perfection. Consider this mission as one of your most urgent responsibilities at the present time. As you well know, it calls for concerted pastoral action in every field of human diligence, economic, cultural and social. If simultaneous progress is made in these various fields, then the intimate life of parents and children in the family will be rendered not only more tolerable, but easier and more joyful. And life together in human society will be enriched with fraternal charity and made more stable with true peace when God's design which He conceived for the world is faithfully followed.

A Great Work

31. Venerable brothers, beloved sons, all men of good will, great indeed is the work of education, of progress and of charity to which We now summon all of you. And this We do relying on the unshakable teaching of the Church, which teaching Peter's successor together with his brothers in the Catholic episcopate faithfully guards and interprets. And We are convinced that this truly great work will bring blessings both on the world and on the Church. For man cannot attain that true happiness for which he yearns with all the strength of his spirit, unless he keeps the laws which the Most High God has engraved in his very nature. These laws must be wisely and lovingly observed. On this great work, on all of you and especially on married couples, We implore from the God of all holiness and pity an abundance of heavenly grace as a pledge of which We gladly bestow Our apostolic blessing.

Given at St. Peter's, Rome, on the 25th day of July, the feast of St. James the Apostle, in the year 1968, the sixth of Our pontificate.

PAUL VI

NOTES

LATIN TEXT: *Acta Apostolicae Sedis*, 60 (1968), 481-503.

ENGLISH TRANSLATION: *The Pope Speaks*, 13 (Fall. 1969), 329-46.

REFERENCES:

(1) See Pius IX, encyc. letter *Oui pluribus: Pii IX P.M. Acta*, 1, pp. 9-10; St. Pius X encyc. letter *Singulari quadam*: AAS 4 (1912), 658; Pius XI, encyc.letter *Casti connubii*: AAS 22 (1930), 579-581; Pius XII, address *Magnificate Dominum* to the episcopate of the Catholic World: AAS 46 (1954), 671-672; *John* XXIII, encyc. letter *Mater et Magistra*: AAS 53 (1961), 457.

(2) See *Mt* 28. 18-19.

(3) See *Mt* 7. 21.

(4) See Council of Trent Roman Catechism, Part II, ch. 8; Leo XIII, encyc.letter *Arcanum*: *Acta Leonis XIII,* 2 (1880), 26-29; Pius XI, encyc.letter *Divini illius Magistri*: AAS 22 (1930), 58-61; encyc. letter *Casti connubii*: AAS 22 (1930), 545-546; Pius XII, Address to Italian Medico-Biological Union of St. Luke: *Discorsi e radiomessaggi di Pio XII*, VI, 191-192; to Italian Association of Catholic Midwives: AAS 43 (1951), 835-854; to the association known as the Family Campaign, and other family associations: AAS 43 (1951), 857-859; to 7th congress of International Society of Hematology: AAS 50 (1958), 734-735 [TPS VI, 394-395]; John XXIII, encyc.letter *Mater et Magistra*: AAS 53 (1961), 446-447 [TPS VII, 330-331]; Second Vatican Council, *Pastoral Constitution on the Church in the World of Today*, nos. 47-52: AAS 58

(1966), 1067-1074 [TPS XI, 289-295]; Code of Canon Law, canons 1067, 1068 §1, canon 1076, §§1-2.

(5) See Paul VI, Address to Sacred College of Cardinals: AAS 56 (1964), 588 [TPS IX, 355-356]; to Commission for the Study of Problems of Population, Family and Birth: AAS 57 (1965), 388 [TPS X, 225]; to National Congress of the Italian Society of Obstetrics and Gynecology: AAS 58 (1966), 1168 [TPS XI, 401-403].

(6) See 1 *Jn* 4. 8.

(7) *Eph* 3. 15.

(8) Second Vatican Council, *Pastoral Constitution on the Church in the World of Today*, no. 50: AAS 58 (1966), 1070-1072 [TPS XI, 292-293].

(9) See St. Thomas, *Summa Theologiae*, I-II, q. 94, art. 2.

(10) See Second Vatican Council, *Pastoral Constitution on the Church in the World of Today*, nos . 50- 5 1: AAS 58 (1 966) 1070-1073 [TPS XI, 292-293].

(11) See *ibid.*, no. 49: AAS 58 (1966), 1070 [TPS XI, 291-292].

(12) See Pius XI. encyc. letter *Casti connubi*: AAS 22 (1930), 560; Pius XII, Address to Midwives: AAS 43 (1951), 843.

(13) See encyc. letter *Mater et Magistra*: AAS 53 (1961), 447 [TPS VII, 331].

(14) See Council of Trent Roman Catechism, Part II, ch. 8; Pius XI, encyc. letter *Casti connubii*: AAS 22 (1930), 562-564; Pius XII, Address to Medico-Biological Union of St. Luke: *Discorsi e radiomessaggi*, VI, 191-192; Address to Midwives: AAS 43 (1951), 842-843; Address to Family Campaign and other family associations: AAS 43 (1951), 857-859; John XXIII, encyc. letter *Pacem in terris*: AAS 55 (1963), 259-260 [TPS IX, 15-16]; Second Vatican Council, *Pastoral*

Constitution on the Church in the World of Today, no. 51: AAS 58 (1966), 1072 [TPS XI, 293].

(15) See Pius XI, encyc. letter *Casti connubii*: AAS 22 (1930), 565; Decree of the Holy Office, Feb. 22, 1940: AAS 32 (1940), 73; Pius XII, Address to Midwives: AAS 43

(1951), 843-844; to the Society of Hematology: AAS 50 (1958), 734-735 [TPS VI, 394-395].

(16) See Council of Trent Roman Catechism, Part II, ch. 8; Pius XI, encyc. letter *Casti connubii*: AAS 22 (1930), 559-561; Pius XII, Address to Midwives: AAS 43 (1951), 843; to the Society of Hematology: AAS 50 (1958), 734-735 [TPS VI, 394-395]; John XXIII, encyc.letter *Mater et Magistra*: AAS 53 (1961), 447 [TPS VII, 331].

(17) See Pius XII, Address to National Congress of Italian Society of the Union of Catholic Jurists: AAS 45 (1953), 798-799 [TPS I, 67-69].

(18) See *Rom* 3. 8.

(19) See Pius XII, Address to 26th Congress of Italian Association of Urology: AAS 45 (1953), 674-675; to Society of Hematology: AAS 50 (1958), 734-735 [TPS VI, 394-395].

(20) See Pius XII, Address to Midwives: AAS 43 (1951), 846.

(21) See Pius XII, Address to Association of Urology: AAS 45 (1953), 674-675; to leaders and members of Italian Association of Cornea Donors and Italian Association for the Blind: AAS 48 (1956), 461-462 [TPS III, 200-201].

(22) *Lk* 2. 34.

(23) See Paul VI, encyc. letter *Populorum progressio*: AAS 59 (1967), 268 [TPS XII, 151].

(24) See *Rom* 8.

(25) See Second Vatican Council, *Decree on the Media of Social Communication*, nos. 6-7: AAS 56 (1964), 147 [TPS IX, 340-341].

(26) Encyc. letter *Mater et Magistra*: AAS 53 (1961), 447 [TPS VII, 331].

(27) See encyc. letter *Populorum progressio*, nos. 48-55: AAS 59 (1967), 281-284 [TPS XII, 160-162].

(28) Second Vatican Council, *Pastoral Constitution on the Church in the World of Today*, no. 52: AAS 58 (1966), 1074 [TPS XI, 294].

(29) Address to Family Campaign and other family associations: AAS 43 (1951), 859.

(30) Second Vatican Council, *Pastoral Constitution on the Church in the World of Today*, no. 51: AAS 58 (1966), 1072 [TPS XI, 293].

(31) See *Mt* 11. 30.

(32) See Second Vatican Council, *Pastoral Constitution on the Church in the World of Today*, no. 48: AAS 58 (1966), 1067-1069 [TPS XI, 290-291]; *Dogmatic Constitution on the Church*, no. 35: AAS 57 (1965), 40-41 [TPS X, 382-383].

(33) *Mt* 7. 14; see *Heb* 12. 11.

(34) See *Ti* 2. 12.

(35) See 1 *Cor* 7. 31.

(36) *Rom* 5. 5.

(37) *Eph* 5. 25, 28-29, 32-33.

(38) See Second Vatican Council, *Dogmatic Constitution on the Church*, nos. 35, 41: AAS 57 (1965), 40-45 [TPS X, 382-383, 386-387; *Pastoral Constitution on the Church in the*

World of Today, nos. 48-49: AAS 58 (1966),1067-1070 [TPS XI, 290-292]; *Decree on the Apostolate of the Laity*, no. 11: AAS 58 (1966), 847-849 [TPS XI, 128-129].

(39) See Second Vatican Council, *Dogmatic Constitution on the Church*, no. 25: AAS 57 (1965), 29-31 [TPS X, 375-376].

(40) 1 *Cor* 1. 10.

(41) See *Jn* 3. 17.

www.ingramcontent.com/pod-product-compliance
Lightning Source LLC
Chambersburg PA
CBHW021151080526
44588CB00008B/290